What Makes the Grand Canyon Grand?

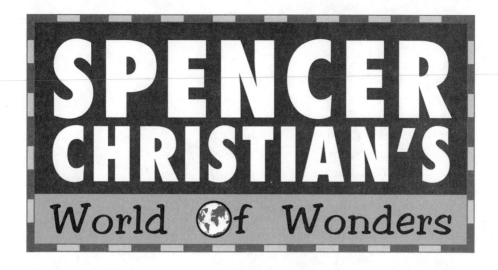

SPENCER
CHRISTIAN'S
World Of Wonders

What Makes the Grand Canyon Grand?

THE WORLD'S MOST AWE-INSPIRING NATURAL WONDERS

Spencer Christian
and Antonia Felix

JOHN WILEY & SONS, INC.
New York • Chichester • Weinheim • Brisbane • Singapore • Toronto

This text is printed on acid-free paper.

Copyright © 1998 by Spencer Christian and Antonia Felix.
Published by John Wiley & Sons, Inc.
Design by Pronto Design & Production Inc.
Illustrations: © 1998 Abe Blashko for the illustrations on pages ix, x, 1, 2, 5, 8, 12, 13, 15, 16, 17, 28, 30, 35, 36, 37, 38, 39, 41, 43, 47, 49, 51, 53, 54, 58, 61, 65, 67, 74, 76, 78, 81, 82, 85, 89, 90, 91, 94, 99, 100, 101, 102, 103, 104, 105 and 106, and © 1998 Jessica Wolk-Stanley for the illustrations on pages 4, 6, 7, 9, 11, 18, 19, 21, 23, 24, 25, 26, 27, 29, 30, 31, 32, 33, 39, 40, 55, 56, 58, 59, 62, 67, 68, 69, 71, 72, 79, 83, 85, 86, 87, 92 and 93.

The publisher and the author have made every reasonable effort to insure that the experiments and activities in the book are safe when conducted as instructed but assume no responsibility for any damage caused or sustained while performing the experiments or activities in the book. Parents, guardians, and/or teachers should supervise young readers who undertake the experiments and activities in this book.

Library of Congress Cataloging-in-Publication Data
Christian, Spencer.
    What makes the Grand Canyon grand?: the world's most awe-inspiring natural wonders / Spencer Christian and Antonia Felix.
        p.   cm — (Spencer Christian's world of wonders)
    Includes index.
    Summary: Focuses on seven of the world's most famous natural wonders including Mount Everest, Victoria Falls, Grand Canyon, Carlsbad Caverns, Giant Redwoods, Paricutín Volcano, and the Nile River.
    ISBN 0-471-19617-7 (pbk. : alk. paper)
    1. Landforms—Juvenile literature. 2. Natural monuments—Juvenile literature. [1. Landforms. 2. Natural monuments.] I. Felix, Antonia. II. Title. III. Series: Christian, Spencer. Spencer Christian's world of wonders.
    GB401.5.C54 1998
    551.41–dc21   97-29470

Printed in the United States of America
10 9 8 7 6 5 4 3 2 1

*This book is dedicated to all teachers
whose lifework is to develop in children
an appreciation for our world of wonders.*

—S. C. and A. F.

Contents

Introduction

MOTHER NATURE, WORLD'S GREATEST ARCHITECT

In New York City, some of the tallest buildings in the world rise up from the concrete and seem to reach the clouds. Majestic skyscrapers are wonders of the modern world, but nothing can top the wonders made by Mother Nature. Glaciers scrape along the ground with a force nothing on Earth can stop. Mountains emerge and volcanoes erupt in mighty natural movements no human-made bulldozer or tank can match. Water, which seems soft and light when you cup rainwater in your hands, has the power to carve giant canyons and to cut permanent riverbeds deep through Earth's rocky surface. Earth's great forests run an air-recycling machine more complex, delicate, and exquisite than any computer could invent or manage.

So what's the story behind Earth's natural wonders, such as the depths of the Grand Canyon and the summits of Mount Everest? In this book, we'll journey to the world's most awesome natural wonders and discover the amazing feats of nature that make this planet a beautiful and unique place in the universe!

Many explorers and world travelers have made lists of the natural wonders that they consider the most awe-inspiring. Here is my list of seven of the world's most famous natural wonders, described in this book:

Seven Natural Wonders of the World

Mount Everest (Nepal/Tibet)

Victoria Falls (Zambia/Zimbabwe)

Grand Canyon (U.S.A.)

Carlsbad Caverns (U.S.A.)

Giant Redwoods (U.S.A.)

Paricutín Volcano (Mexico)

Nile River (Egypt)

Other natural wonders often listed are the northern lights, Australia's Great Barrier Reef, and Brazil's harbor of Rio de Janeiro, and we will discover many more notable wonders throughout this book—amazing sights carved out of nature's own creativity and power.

Canyons

CARVING THE EARTH

Whenever it rains, the rainwater moves downhill, no matter how slight the slope may be. Pulled by *gravity* (the force that pulls objects toward Earth's center), water always seeks the lowest ground. Rainwater that falls on your front lawn moves toward lower ground at your street. Rain on streets pours into drains that channel the water into a nearby river or ocean. A storm in the mountains sends rain tumbling rapidly down the mountain slopes into streams and rivers.

As water runs along the ground, it picks up small, loose objects that flow along until the *current* (movement of the water) is no longer strong enough to carry them. In the moving water, sand and pebbles bump into other objects, shake them loose, and send them flowing into the current, too. The steeper the slope, the faster the water moves. Over millions of years, fast-moving water has dug out huge river valleys from solid rock. The process of wearing down rock by water or wind is **erosion.** A steep, narrow river valley is a **canyon.**

Copper Canyon

The biggest group of canyons in the world is in the Mexican state of Chihuahua, where rivers have cut 20 canyons through an area about four times **bigger** than America's Grand Canyon. These canyons, covering 10,000 square miles (25,000 square kilo-meters [sq. km]), were carved out by rivers running down the Sierra Madre mountains. Together, the entire region is called "Copper Canyon." The canyons tower up from three main rivers: the Urique, the Río Verde, and the Batopilas. The canyon near the town of Batopilas measures 6,900 feet, or $1\frac{1}{3}$ miles (2,100 m), deep. The canyons on these three rivers are the second, third, and fourth deepest in North America. The deepest canyon on the continent is Hell's Canyon on the border of Idaho and Oregon, which has a depth of about 7,900 feet (2,409 m). The Copper Canyon region got its name from the copper that was mined there in the 1800s.

Raramuri: World-Famous Canyon Runners

The hot, dry, and rocky Copper Canyon region—filled with cliffs, mountains, and deep valleys—is not an easy place to explore. Yet for more than 500 years, it has been home to the native Tarahumaras, who are known throughout the world as great runners. The only way to get around the mountains and canyons is to walk or run, and all Tarahumara children, boys and girls, learn to run easily across the rugged land. The Tarahumara call themselves the "Raramuri," which means the "runners." Raramuri men can run 100 miles (160 km) without stopping! That's the same as if I sprinted out of the *Good Morning America* TV studio in New York City and ran non-stop to Philadelphia! Raramuri men can hunt a deer by chasing it for so long that the deer stops, exhausted, and can be easily killed. Raramuri men have been members of Mexico's Olympic running team. At the 1992 Leadville Trail 100, America's most rugged marathon race, two Raramuri runners finished in first and second place—running in leather sandals. The first-place winner was 55 years old.

The Grand Canyon: A View into Earth's Rocky History

In 1540, Spanish explorer García Lopez de Cárdenas was riding west out of the mountains that are now called the "Rockies." He was a scout for explorer Francisco de Coronado, the first European to travel to the southwestern region of North America. Cárdenas and his band of explorers rode into a spectacle unlike anything they had ever imagined. As far as the eye could see, huge cliffs cut deep into the earth, from ground level. The cliffs were striped with layers of red, purple, and other colors of rock, which glowed brightly in the hot sun. Cárdenas had discovered the Grand Canyon.

For the next 300 years, the Grand Canyon would remain a mystery to the rest of the world until another explorer came along. In 1869, John Wesley Powell, a teacher and Civil War veteran, led nine men on the first American expedition through the canyon. Powell was also a *geologist*, a scientist who studies rocks, soil, and the structure of Earth. Following each of his trips into the canyon, he carried out a great deal of knowledge to curious scientists and other people who read about Powell's discoveries in journals and magazines.

How to Make a Canyon

Since Powell's trips into the canyon and his daring raft rides on the powerful Colorado River that runs along its bottom, many other geologists have studied it. They have learned that the rock exposed at the bottom of the canyon is ancient, nearly 2 billion years old. The canyon itself is not nearly that old. The Colorado River did not begin to carve out the canyon until about 6 million years ago. How could one river slice through so much rock?

Over millions of years, the Colorado River carved out the Grand Canyon.

Moving water causes erosion, and the Colorado River has always been a very fast-moving river. When the Rocky Mountains sprang up about 60 million years ago, rainfall began to form into small streams along the mountainsides. Twenty million years ago, these streams formed the Colorado River. Flowing down the western side of the mountains, the Colorado began to erode the rock and to form the oldest canyon in the Grand Canyon system, Marble Canyon.

The rocky surface of Earth that the Colorado River carved into Marble Canyon was made up of limestone, sandstone, and shale. These types of rock are *permeable:* They are filled with tiny holes through which water can enter and flow out again. Limestone erodes much more quickly than a harder type of rock, such as granite, which does not have very many spaces or cracks in it. As it crashed across the land, the Colorado began to eat away at the somewhat soft rock.

About 17 million years ago, events deep within Earth sped up the whole canyon-making process. For reasons that geologists do not fully understand, a vast stretch of land west of the Rocky Mountains, now called the "Colorado Plateau," began to rise. This land gently slopes down toward the south, like a giant tabletop that has been tilted. The new slope of the land made the Colorado River run even faster on its way to the Pacific Ocean. Erosion sped up, and canyons grew even deeper.

The inside of the Grand Canyon is hot and dry throughout the year. Heat and sun bake the ground, and when rain falls, it can't soak into the hard ground. A heavy rainfall in the canyon can quickly cause a large buildup of water on the surface, called a "flash flood," which washes down the canyon. Crashing down the side of a cliff, a flash flood can move huge boulders and anything else that gets in its way. In a desert, none of the plants have deep roots to hold the soil in place, so the force of a flash flood can break the soil loose and carry it away.

Water also causes erosion when it turns to ice. In winter months, the north edge of the canyon can get very cold at night, even though it's a desert. Water that seeps into cracks in the rock can freeze. When water freezes, it expands and forces the cracks in the rock to spread apart. Wind and water can whip through those cracks and further break down the rock. Eventually, a rock

CRACK-UP!

On the Grand Canyon's north rim and on the peaks of mountains, ice breaks up rock. This activity explores the cracking effect of freezing water.

What You Need:
- Freezer

- 2 sticks of modeling clay

- Plastic wrap

- Water

What to Do:

1. Moisten your hands with water, and roll each stick of clay into a damp ball. Remoisten your hands a couple of times while you roll the clay, so the balls are slippery on the outside.
2. Wrap both balls in plastic wrap.
3. Put one ball in the freezer, and set the other one aside.
4. Wait 24 hours, then remove the ball from the freezer.
5. Unwrap both balls, and compare them.
6. Remoisten the ball that had been frozen, wrap it again, and return it to the freezer.
7. After another 24 hours, unwrap the frozen ball, and observe what happened.

What Happens and Why:
Cracks appear in the frozen ball wherever water has seeped into the clay. The cracks are created when the water freezes. The water expands as it freezes, and it pushes against the clay. When the ice melts, it leaves behind cracks in the clay. The ball that was set aside at room temperature did not crack.

The Colorado Plateau: Land of Amazing Natural Sculptures

Over millions of years, water and wind have carved fascinating structures throughout the Colorado Plateau. Sculptures of stone include graceful *arches*, created when entire blocks fall away from a large rock. Water and wind seep into *joints* (cracks) in the rock. Over millions of years, the joints are wide enough to allow large pieces of rock to break off. When blocks break through the width of a rock, a *window* is formed with an arch hanging over the top. The biggest collection of natural arches in the world is found in Utah's Arches National Park. In 1940, the park's Skyline Arch doubled in size when a huge block fell away.

When wind and water wear away soft rock to expose the harder rock beneath, the erosion sculpts *hoodoos* (pillars). Along the Catalina Highway near Tucson stand hoodoos made of hard granite rock, in shapes that look like elephants, hams, and weird human profiles!

Another fascinating natural sculpture found on the Colorado Plateau is a *balanced-rock* structure. As rocks erode, cracks within them widen.

Natural wonders sculpted on the Colorado Plateau include arches, hoodoos, balanced rocks, and mesas.

Arch

Hoodoo

Balanced rock

Mesa

Sometimes, a large wall of rock becomes split up into several columns. When two blocks of hard rock are stacked up, separated by a layer of softer rock, the soft rock eventually erodes away and leaves the top block balanced on top of the bottom one. A stack of these odd-looking blocks creates a bizarre column that gradually breaks apart as erosion does its endless work on rock.

continued

The Colorado Plateau *(continued)*

Another group of strange towers on the plateau are the *spires* of Arizona's Chiricahua National Monument. This cluster of spires was formed by colossal volcanic eruptions 25 million years ago. Lava and ash shot down the ancient volcano slopes and immediately hardened into rock called "welded tuff."

When a *dike* (a strip of rock) is exposed through erosion, it appears on the landscape as a wall of rock. A dike is formed when *magma* (melted rock inside of Earth) seeps up into a vertical crack of rock. When the magma cools, it hardens into a very hard type of rock. The rock surrounding the dike can then be worn away through erosion, thus exposing the dike and making it part of the landscape. Ridges of dikes that stretch for several miles can be found near Tuba City in Arizona.

Another common site on the plateau is the *mesa,* a steep-sided mountain or hill with a flat top. The top of the mesa is made of *caprock* (a layer of hard rock that resists erosion). The rock beneath the caprock is shielded from water and wind erosion and remains standing when erosion cuts away the rock beyond it. A small mesa is a *butte.*

Caprock is also found on the top of narrow columns of rock that have been sculpted by erosion. These columns are made of harder stone than the limestone and shale that once surrounded them. After the water eroded all the surrounding softer rock, the harder rock remained in the shape of a pillar, tower, spire, or other shape.

at the edge of a cliff will be cracked enough to push the rock over the edge. As a rock falls down the canyon, it **loosens** other rocks along the way and causes many to fall. In a flash flood, the fallen rocks are swept away to the Colorado River.

The Glen Canyon Dam, built to hold back the Colorado River in the spring and to prevent floods in Arizona, has slowed the river's movement through the canyon. As a result, the erosion of the Grand Canyon has slowed down. Also, the river has reached a layer of very hard rock, granite and schist, which is much more difficult to erode.

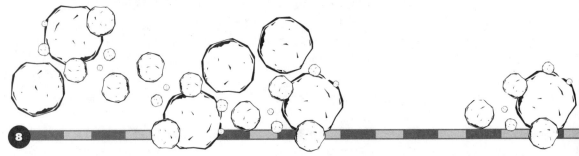

MAKE ROCK SCULPTURES

Throughout the Colorado Plateau are odd-shaped structures that have been carved by water and wind erosion. In this experiment, we'll use sand and pennies to observe how erosion wears away soft material to create towers of hard material.

What You Need:
- A plastic or glass plate

- 2 cups (0.5 liter) sand

- 15 pennies

- A rainy day or a watering can and some newspapers

What to Do:
1. Arrange the pennies in three stacks of five coins each.
2. Place the stacks of pennies on the plate, near the center, about 1 inch (2.54 cm) apart.
3. Gently pour the sand over the center of the dish, covering each stack of coins.
4. On a rainy day, place the plate outside, where rain will fall on it. After a few minutes, bring the plate inside. If there's no rain, put the plate on a layer of newspapers on a table. Pour a full watering can over the sand.

What Happens and Why:
The rain seeped into the mound of sand and washed it away. The stacks of pennies remained standing. Water erosion breaks down softer rock, such as limestone and shale, more quickly than it does harder rock, such as granite. This process is how erosion creates rock sculptures on the Colorado Plateau.

Grand Canyon by the Numbers

The portion of the Colorado River that forms the Grand Canyon is 277 miles (446 km) long. At its deepest, the canyon extends 6,000 feet (1,829 km) from its rim to the river. At its widest, it stretches across 18 miles (29 km).

A Museum of Earth History

To descend into the Grand Canyon is to go back in time, step by step, through nearly 2 billion years of Earth history. Each layer of rock represents a chapter in the formation of the land. More than 15 distinct layers of rock line the walls of the Grand Canyon. Each one **unlocks** an era of Earth history, a time line of life on the planet, captured in the stone. Near the rim are the remains of objects made by canyon-dwelling humans, such as pots and tools, which date back 12,000 years. Deeper down are dinosaur fossils, and deeper still are traces of tiny, one-celled life-forms. At the very bottom is rock nearly 2 billion years old—about half as old as the planet itself!

The oldest rock, at the bottom of the canyon, is darkly colored. This ancient rock layer was squeezed and folded by miles of rock piled on top of it more than 2 billion years ago, long before the present layers of the canyon were formed. One of the oldest layers, called the "Bass Formation," contains fossils of ancient *algae* (simple plants) that lived in coastal waters about 1.25 billion years ago.

Over millions of years, seas have filled up the southwestern United States and dried up again several times. Each time the sea dries up, it leaves behind a thick layer of minerals, sand, and other bits of rock, called "sediment." With each new life cycle of an inland sea, a new layer of sediment is formed. The weight of each new layer causes the layers below to squeeze together and harden into rock.

Sometimes the rock layer at the surface is completely washed away by water and wind erosion. How do scientists know that a layer is missing, or was completely washed away? They figure out the ages of each rock layer, and when the dated ages of two rock layers next to each other have a gap between them they know they're missing a layer. A missing layer of rock in a canyon is an **unconformity**. Although the seas have not returned recently, the entire canyon is still changing through wind and water erosion.

tanding out brightly in vivid orange-red colors just above the Bass Formation is a rock layer called the "Hakatai Shale." Above it is another ancient layer formed by sea sediment, the Dox Formation. In this layer, water flowed over sand, creating ripples in the sand, which hardened into rock about 1.19 billion years ago. Above the Dox Formation, the Muav Limestone layer was created as the floor of a shallow sea about 530 million years ago. Just above it is a very thick layer of Redwall Limestone, which was formed when the land was under the sea for about 30 million years. Above the Redwall layer are layers of sandstone and shale, called "Hermit Shale" and the "Supai Group." These higher layers contain *iron oxide*, a red-colored mineral that works as a red *pigment* (substance that gives color to something). The red pigment then **seeps down** into the Redwall layer. Finally, at the top of the canyon is another limestone layer, which is about 250 million years old. Geologists know that this rock, called the "Kaibab Limestone," was formed at the bottom of a sea because it contains many fossils of tiny sea creatures. Any rock layers that may have been created less than 250 million years ago have been completely worn away by erosion.

The top layer of rock at the Grand Canyon is about 250 million years old, while the rock found at the deepest, oldest layer is about 1.7 billion years old.

Oldest Rock
(1.7 billion
years old)

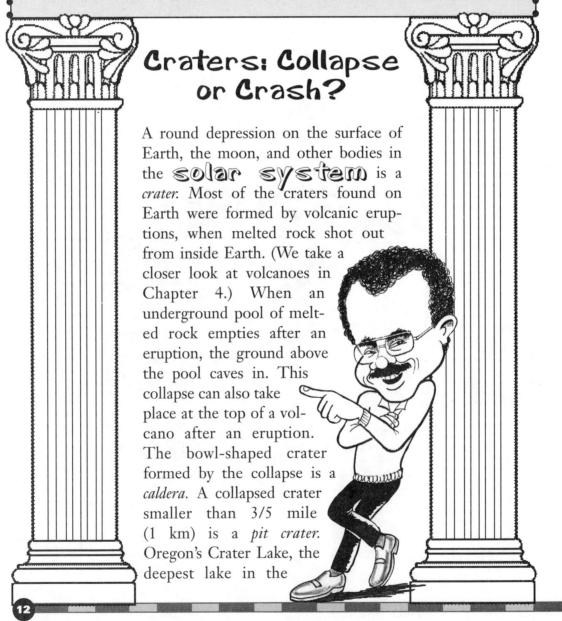

The Strange Forms of Utah's Canyon-lands

In southeastern Utah, the Green and Colorado Rivers have carved out canyons, arches, and many other formations. One section, called the "Needles," is filled with massive red and white pillars made of eroded sandstone. Geologists haven't discovered exactly how one structure, Upheaval Dome, was created. This 2-mile-wide (3.2 km) dish of rock is framed by a ring of raised rock. Because it looks like a crater, some geologists think it was created by a *meteorite* (a meteor that reaches the surface of a planet) that crashed to Earth long ago.

Craters: Collapse or Crash?

A round depression on the surface of Earth, the moon, and other bodies in the solar system is a *crater*. Most of the craters found on Earth were formed by volcanic eruptions, when melted rock shot out from inside Earth. (We take a closer look at volcanoes in Chapter 4.) When an underground pool of melted rock empties after an eruption, the ground above the pool caves in. This collapse can also take place at the top of a volcano after an eruption. The bowl-shaped crater formed by the collapse is a *caldera*. A collapsed crater smaller than 3/5 mile (1 km) is a *pit crater*. Oregon's Crater Lake, the deepest lake in the

The World's First Apartment Buildings—Canyon Cliff Dwellers

From about 100 B.C. to A.D. 1,500, a group of very gifted stone builders lived in the Canyon de Chelly in New Mexico. The Anasazi (Ancient Ones), ancestors of the modern-day Pueblo Indians who live in the American Southwest, created houses made of rock and mud along the cliffs of the canyon. These beautifully designed houses were often two or three stories high and arranged in clusters. The dry climate of the canyon has preserved thousands of the Anasazi cliff dwellings, some of which can be visited today. No one knows why these people, who lived by farming corn, beans, and squash, left the canyon nearly 500 years ago.

United States, was formed about 7,700 years ago, when the top of the volcano Mount Mazama collapsed.

Most craters in the solar system, however, are formed from outer-space action. An *impact crater* is created when a large meteorite or other space object collides with a planet or a moon. All the craters on Earth's moon are impact craters, and some of them are so big you can see them without the help of binoculars or a telescope. Earth has fewer impact craters than the moon because most meteors burn up in Earth's atmosphere. In Arizona, Meteor Crater was formed by the crash of a meteorite 49,000 years ago. The collision left a dent in Earth 3 miles (48 km) around and 470 feet (143 m) deep.

When a meteor or other space object breaks up into several pieces before striking a planet, it forms a *crater chain* (series of craters). A spectacular crater-chain impact occurred on Jupiter in 1992. Captured on film by the Hubble Telescope, the entire world watched as a huge *comet* (a space object made up of dust and gas) broke apart, crashed to the planet surface, and created a series of giant explosions. Crater chains can also be found on Earth. Eight craters form a 435-mile (700-km) line across Missouri and Illinois. Scientists have dated these craters to be about 300 million years old. In Africa, a meteor collision about 360 million years ago caused three craters in a row, in northern Chad.

2

Wild Waters
RIVERS, RAPIDS, AND WATERFALLS

What do Minneapolis, Minnesota, United States; London, England; Paris, France; Budapest, Hungary; Delhi, India; and Cairo, Egypt; have in common? Like many of the major cities of the world, each of these places was settled alongside a river. When people first began to grow crops and form farming societies several thousand years ago, they chose to live by rivers. The river gave almost everything needed for survival, from freshwater for drinking and fresh fish for eating to moist land for growing crops. In ancient Egypt, people used the water of the Nile to *irrigate* (provide water for) their crops as early as 3,400 B.C. These groups of farmers developed into the Egyptian *civilization* (organized society) on land that is now the city of Cairo. About 2,400 years ago, a tribe of fishers called the "Parisii" settled in France on a small island in the Seine river. The city of Paris grew out of that farming society. At about the same time, farmers and fishers began to settle along a small stretch of the river Thames (pronounced "temz") in England, and London was born.

Trickle to Tributary: The Life of a River

A *river* is a body of freshwater that flows in a definite channel. River water comes from rainwater, lakes, springs, or **melting** ice and snow. The place where a river begins is the **river source.** The source of a river, on a mountain or hill, may start as a **rill** (a tiny, narrow channel of rainwater). As rills run into each other and get larger, they become *brooks.* A series of brooks traveling down the mountain flow together to form a *stream.* Fast-flowing streams pick up **silt** (fine particles of soil). Streams then empty into a larger body of water, such as a lake or a river. The small channels that make up the source of a river (its rills, brooks, and streams) are **headwaters.**

Russia's great Volga River begins as a series of streams in the Valdai Hills in western Russia. The source of the mighty Mississippi River of the United States is a small stream pouring out of Lake Itasca in northern Minnesota. The Rhône River that runs from Switzerland to the Mediterranean Sea starts out as melted water from a glacier high in the mountains of the Alps.

The scooped-out valley through which river water runs is the river **channel.** At the bottom of the channel is the **riverbed,** and along its edges are the **river banks.** Near the source of the river, the slope of the land tends to be steep. The **river mouth,** where the river drains into the ocean, runs on flat land. Rivers flow fast near the source as they rush to lower ground, then they slow down when they reach low-lying level land.

Small rivers, called **tributaries,** feed into larger rivers. Large rivers, together with their tributaries, make up river systems that drain water from large areas of land. They then pour the water into oceans. The region of Earth drained by a river system is a **river basin.** In South America, the Amazon River basin (called "Amazonia") covers about **one third** of that entire continent. From the Andes Mountains on the west coast, the Amazon's river system drains the water from 2.7 million square miles (7 million sq. km) of land into the Atlantic Ocean. The Mississippi River drains about 40 percent of the land area of the United States (not including Alaska and Hawaii).

Earth's Drain

Rivers drain about 60 percent of Earth's land surface. Other water soaks into the ground, *evaporates* (changes from liquid water into water vapor), or is frozen in glaciers.

Rainwater and meltwater from snow and ice flow down both sides of a mountain range. Along the very top of the range, an imaginary line called the **drainage divide** separates the mountainsides into two basins. One river basin flows down one side, and the other basin flows down the other side. In the western United States, the drainage divide on top of the Rocky Mountains is the *Continental Divide.* Water flowing down the west side flows into rivers that take it to the Pacific Ocean. Water flowing down the east side enters rivers that stretch to the Atlantic Ocean, the Arctic Ocean, or the Gulf of Mexico.

On level ground, a river begins to flow more slowly. The flat land through which it flows is a **floodplain.** During a flood, when a river overflows its banks, this flat region becomes covered by water. When the flood waters *recede* (dry up, uncovering the land around the

STIR UP A STREAM!

When a stream moves quickly, it breaks off tiny particles of the land over which it flows. Rivers heavy with silt look brown, but rivers containing only small amounts of silt are clear. The silt in China's Huang (Yellow) River contains a yellow mineral that gives the river a yellowish color. In this activity, we'll create a fast-moving stream and observe what it does to the soil of the streambed.

What You Need:
- 3 cups (0.72 liters) sand

- Clean, empty 16-ounce (0.47 liter) mayonnaise jar

- Large round mixing bowl

- Water

- Soup spoon

What to Do:
1. Fill the mayonnaise jar with 2.5 cups (0.6 liters) of sand. This weighs the jar down so that it won't move.
2. Place the jar in the center of the bowl.
3. Pour water into the bowl until it is about halfway up to the top of the jar.
4. Sprinkle the rest of the sand into the bowl in a thin, even layer.
5. Stir the water slowly with the spoon.
6. Pick up your stirring speed, and create a moving current in the bowl.

What Happens and Why:
When you stirred slowly, your current was not strong enough to pick up any sand. When you stirred faster, your stream picked up some of the sand and pushed some of it into little ridges. Just like a stream moving down a hill or a mountain, your stream-in-a-bowl picked up silt.

river), bits of rock, sand, and sediment are left behind on the land next to the river. This material forms a **natural levee,** a buildup of land. In very moist regions, the land behind the natural levee forms a **swamp,** a wet area of land.

A floodplain can extend for hundreds of miles (or kilometers). As a river channel flows over its flood plain, it curves from side to side. These snake-like moves create bends in the river, called "meanders." When the floodwater recedes, some of the loops are cut off from the rest of the river. Water left behind in a bend forms an **oxbow lake,** a crescent-shaped body of water.

When a river nears an ocean, it drops off the silt and bits of rock it has been carrying onto a **delta,** a flat area next to the sea. This delta region forms into a smooth, fan-shaped area, undisturbed by great waves or strong tides. The material deposited in the delta is the **river load.**

The river load forming each delta is very fertile because it is filled with minerals that help crops and other plants grow. In Egypt, India, Pakistan, Vietnam, and other countries, millions of people live and grow food on delta land. One large rice-growing region in

A river system drains water from a large area of land.

Spring Stream
Rapids
Divide
Tributary
Oxbow lake
Levee Meander
Mouth
Swamp Flood plain

Rivers That Build a Nation

The Netherlands, a country on the coast of northern Europe, is a large delta made by the Rhine, Meuse, and Scheldt Rivers.

Vietnam is formed by the Mekong River, which flows from China through Southeast Asia. The mouth of this river forms a vast delta on the southeast coast of Vietnam, where the river flows into the South China Sea.

The mouth of a river does not always end in a delta. Some rivers meet the sea through an **estuary,** a deep, broad river mouth. When the sea level was lower, the estuary was a typical river channel cut into a valley. When the sea level rose, however, it filled the valley and flooded the mouth of the river. An estuary is a mix of freshwater from a river and salt water from an ocean. One of the world's biggest estuaries is at the mouth of the Amazon River in South America. From bank to bank, the river's entrance to the ocean is about 167 miles (270 km) wide.

All Dried Up

A river that is sometimes completely dry and fills up again only when it rains is an **intermittent river.** In Algeria, Israel, and other Middle Eastern countries, intermittent rivers are called "wadis." In the southwestern United States, an intermittent river is called an "arroyo" or a "wash."

The Nile River in Egypt and the Colorado River in the American southwest flow through huge deserts. Why doesn't the water in those rivers dry up? The source of these rivers is on very high ground, where the water is plentiful. Although the rivers cross vast desert regions on their way to the sea, they contain plenty of water to keep flowing across hundreds of miles of desert without going dry.

Rivers are described as young, mature, or old. One river can be all three at the same time, as these terms refer to particular features of a river as it flows from mountain to sea, not to its age. A *young river* flows rapidly over a steep surface. As water whips down a steep, rocky riverbed filled with boulders, it crashes over the rocks. Ledges of rock form sharp steps, and the fast current smashes into big rocks, forming fearsome **rapids.** For instance, the mighty rapids of the Colorado River, as it cut through the Grand Canyon, challenged the courage and strength of early explorers. Steering a boat through rapids is always dangerous and difficult, and rapids still

PRESSURE SQUIRT!

This experiment uses a tall bottle and some water to demonstrate how water is under more pressure in the deepest part of a river (or any body of water) than it is in shallower parts.

What You Need:
- 2-quart (1.9-liter) plastic bottle

- Nail

- Water

- Tray

- Adult helper

What to Do:
1. Ask an adult to use the nail to make four holes in the bottle, spaced about 1.5 inches (3.8 cm) apart.
2. Cover the holes with your fingers, and hold the bottle beneath the tap at the kitchen sink. Ask a friend to turn on the tap and to fill the bottle with water.
3. Place the bottle in the tray, and remove your fingers.

What Happens and Why:
The four jets of water shoot out at different lengths. The greater the pressure, the longer the stream. The stream at the top is weakest because the water pressure is lowest at the top of the bottle. The jet nearest the bottom shoots out farthest because the water pressure is greatest at the deepest level.

make up a long and treacherous stretch of the young Colorado River. Young rivers also have few tributaries and do not form levees.

A *mature river* has slowed its course and winds across a wide flood plain. The slope of the land is too gentle to form rapids or waterfalls. Tributaries reach the river at this stage, and the mature river develops natural levees and swamps. Even though a mature river does not move fast, it can still have an enormous amount of power. The *pressure of water*—its power to move anything in its path—increases with the river's depth. The deepest part of a river is under great pressure from the **weight** of the water above. This pressure gives the river the power to pick up rocks, sediment, and other materials from the riverbed. Near the ocean or sea, a river is considered old. Moving slowly, it winds through flat floodplains and is likely to form a spreading delta.

The World's 20 Longest Rivers

River	Location	Miles	Km
Nile	Africa	4,150	6,680
Amazon	South America	4,000	6,400
Yangtze	China	3,964	6,380
Huang (Yellow)	Asia	3,028	4,873
Congo	Africa	2,900	4,700
Amur	Asia	2,800	4,500
Paraná	South America	2,700	4,300
Lena	Asia	2,650	4,260
Irtysh	Asia	2,640	4,250
Mackenzie	North America	2,635	4,241
Niger	Africa	2,600	4,200
Yenisey	Asia	2,570	4,140
Missouri	North America	2,540	4,064
Mekong	Asia	2,500	4,000
Mississippi	North America	2,340	3,779
Volga	Europe	2,300	3,700
Ob	Asia	2,290	3,690
Madeira	South America	2,100	3,400
Purus	South America	1,900	3,100
Rio Grande	North America	1,885	3,034

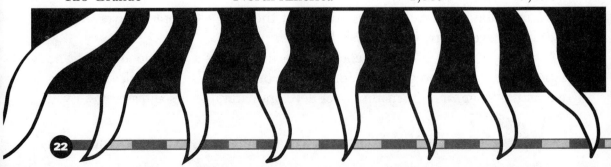

Some Great Rivers up Close

The Nile

In ancient times, people who lived near the Nile River created wonderful civilizations and achieved great things. The Nile River valley is called the "birthplace of civilization." The great scholars of ancient Egypt and Greece could not understand, however, why the Nile flowed north rather than south, like most of the other rivers they had seen. Another big mystery about the Nile that made it seem magical was the fact that it would flood the land in late summer, when the Nile's desert region had not had any rain for months.

In 1862, English explorer J. H. Speke discovered that the Nile begins high in Lake Victoria in the African country of Uganda. The lake is 3,700 feet (1,130 meters [m]) above sea level, and it supplies the water that flows northward down Uganda's sloping land. The world's longest river then plunges northward all the way to Cairo, where it fans out into a vast delta that extends 135 miles (220 km) before emptying into the Medi-

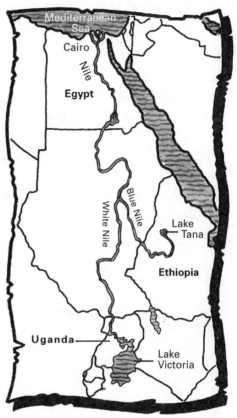

The Nile River in Africa is the longest river in the world.

terranean Sea. As it flows from higher to lower elevation, the Nile sweeps from south to north. That answers mystery number one.

What about the summer flooding? Scientists unlocked this secret in the twentieth century. Two major tributaries flow into the Nile: the Blue Nile and the White Nile. The source of the Blue Nile is in high country in Ethiopia, where the river is fed by Lake Tana and by many streams. In this Ethiopian high country, rain falls heavily in the summer, filling the Blue Nile with rainwater. In late summer, the rain-filled Blue Nile contributes about 63 percent of the total water volume of the Nile and causes the main river to flood.

The Amazon

outh America's Amazon River may be number two in terms of length, but it's **number one** for the amount of water it carries, so it's the mightiest river in the world. The Amazon drains water from more

Naming the Amazon River

In 1541, Spanish explorer Francisco de Orellana was the first European to travel on the Amazon River. His tropical adventure almost ended when Orellana and his group were attacked by native female warriors. The Spanish explorers barely escaped.

Orellana thought that the fierce women may have been descendants of famous women warriors called "Amazons," described in Greek mythology. In memory of his brush with death, he named the river the Amazon.

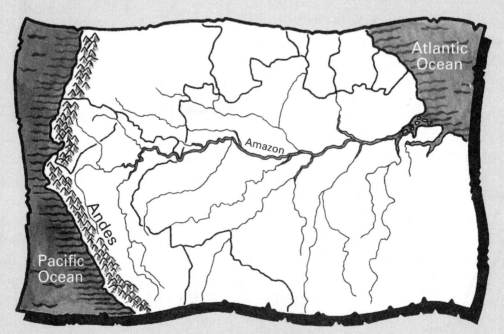

The Amazon River in South America has the largest volume of water of any river.

than one third of the South American continent. Every second, this river pours more than 55 million gallons (200,000 cubic meters) into the Atlantic Ocean. This volume of water is greater than the Nile, the Yangtze (the longest river in China), and the Mississippi Rivers combined. Fed by heavy tropical rains and melting snow in the Andes, the Amazon stretches for 4,000 miles (6,400 km). The river flows from west to east, beginning in the Andes Mountains and gathering water from hundreds of rivers as it sweeps across the continent and empties into the sea. The Amazon winds through one of the most important and awesome land areas in the world, the tropical rain forest, which we explore in Chapter 5.

The mouth of the Amazon is an estuary 167 miles (270 km) wide. The estuary is so wide and deep, huge ships can travel about 1,000 miles (1,609 km) up the Amazon, as far as the Brazilian river port of Manaus. When it flows out from the estuary into the ocean, the immense amount of water in the Amazon can be seen from the air as a muddy trail stretching 200 miles (320 km) out into the sea.

The Yangtze

The world's third largest river flows west to east through China. The Chinese call the river "Chang Kiang" (Long River). Glaciers in the Tangkula and Kunlun Mountains that border China and Tibet form the source of the river. About half the population of China lives in the Yangtze River

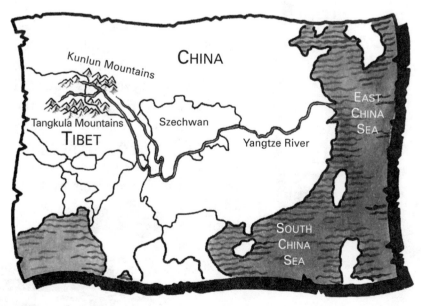

China's Yangtze River is the world's deepest river.

Kunlun Mountains

CHINA

Tangkula Mountains   Szechwan

TIBET   Yangtze River

EAST CHINA SEA

SOUTH CHINA SEA

basin, which drains an area of 700,000 square miles (1.8 million square km) of land. The rushing headwaters of the Yangtze contrast sharply with its calm, broad delta at the East China Sea. The river begins by flowing down rugged mountains, forming rapids and waterfalls. Leaving the mountains, it passes into Szechwan province. At the east end of the province, the Yangtze passes through a famous series of steep valleys called the "Yichang Gorges." At this stage, it is the deepest river in the world, with a channel about 500 to 600 feet (152 to 182 m) deep. The river becomes slow and broad as it nears the *fertile* delta region, which is filled with canals and lakes.

In 1954, the Yangtze flooded its banks in one of the worst flood disasters in history. After heavy rains, the river overflowed and spread across 590 miles (950 km) of land.

The Mississippi

Extending from nearly the top of the United States clear down south to the bottom at the Gulf of Mexico, the Mississippi is the second longest river in North America (the Missouri is the longest, at 2,540 feet [4,064 km]). The source of "Old Man River" is a stream flowing out of Lake Itasca in northwestern Minnesota.

The Mississippi River played an important role in the exploration of the central and western United States. In the 1500s and 1600s, Spanish and French explorers used the river as a major water highway. In the 1800s, steamboats chugged up and down the river and made the Mississippi an important trade route. *Steamboats* are powered by a steam engine and pushed through the water by large paddle wheels in the back of the boat.

The Mississippi River flows nearly the entire length of the United States.

The Greatest Job on the Mississippi

American author Mark Twain grew up in Missouri and spent a lot of time watching the Mississippi River. One of his most famous books describes every detail of river life: *Life on the Mississippi*.

"When I was a boy, there was but one permanent ambition among my comrades in our village on the west bank of the Mississippi River. That was, to be a steamboatman."

Steamboats provided food and supplies to forts and pioneers in frontier territory. They carried furs and other goods from Minneapolis in the north to St. Louis, New Orleans, and other cities in the south.

The Mississippi has three major **tributaries**: the Illinois, the Missouri, and the Ohio Rivers. Where the Ohio River flows into the Mississippi River, at Cairo, Illinois, the Ohio doubles the Mississippi's volume. At that point, the Mississippi is divided into the upper Mississippi (above the Ohio) and the lower Mississippi (below the Ohio). The lower river forms a fertile valley floodplain dotted with oxbow lakes. South of New Orleans, the mouth of the river fans out into a massive delta covering about 13,000 square miles (33,700 square km). The delta is broken up into several channels, called "distributaries," which enter the Gulf of Mexico.

The Volga

With its source in the Valdai Hills of Russia, about 227 miles (365 km) northwest of Moscow, the Volga is the longest river in Europe. Winding southward toward the Caspian Sea, the Volga River basin drains western Russia and most of eastern Europe. The river is affectionately called "Mother Volga" in Russia and has served as the principal waterway of

In The Volga River in Russia, some sections are frozen more than 100 days out of every year.

that country for thousands of years. Timber logged from the forests moves downstream to lumberyards, and grain, flour, oil, salt, fruit, and many other goods from the southern farmlands move upstream to supply the cities. Shipping on the Volga is limited by the cold weather in Russia. The northern section of the river is frozen 150 days out of the year, and even the southern section freezes to a halt 110 days out of the year. The broad delta at the mouth of the Volga is a world-famous fishing area. Many of the fish caught there are valued for their eggs, which are packaged as a delicacy called "caviar."

Waterfalls: Over the Edge

When I first saw Niagara Falls, about 10 years ago, I couldn't figure out what all the fuss was about. From the New York side, I could see the famous falls of the Niagara River, on the border between the United States and Canada, drop over

Niagara Means "Thundering Waters" in the Native Iroquois Language

Niagara Falls are made of two waterfalls, one in the United States and one in Canada.

What causes a river to suddenly drop its channel in one huge step to form a waterfall? As we discovered in the story of canyons (in Chapter 1), moving water breaks up rock in a process called "erosion." When a river flows from an area of very hard rock to one of softer rock, it erodes the soft rock more quickly. The softer rock downstream gradually breaks down, causing the river channel to move down in steep levels. Many waterfalls consist of **cascades,** a series of small falls on top of one another. A waterfall that flows with a very large volume of water is a **cataract.**

Waterfalls are formed in another way on high mountaintops. High mountain falls are often tributary streams that drop down a steep cliff to reach the river below. The cliff makes up one side of a **hanging valley,** a deep channel cut by the river. The river, which is larger and stronger than the streams that feed into it, cuts more quicky into the rock than a small stream can. When a stream meets the deep hanging river valley, it forms a waterfall on its journey to join the river. Mountain waterfalls created by hanging valleys are found in the Alps, in mountains of Norway, and in the glacier mountains of western North America and New Zealand.

Falling water is a powerful force that can be used for producing energy, called "hydroelectric power." To create this electrical power, the water is used to turn large, round machines called "turbines." A hydroelectric

continued

Niagara Means "Thundering Waters" *(continued)*

plant transforms the movement of the turbine into electricity. Often, people construct a *dam,* a structure built to hold back the water above the falls. The dam helps control the amount of water being used to generate power. Half of the water that originally flowed over Niagara Falls is now redirected to a hydroelectric power plant, for use by the United States and Canada. Dams are also used to raise the level of a body of water, thus creating a source of water for irrigating crops and for other uses.

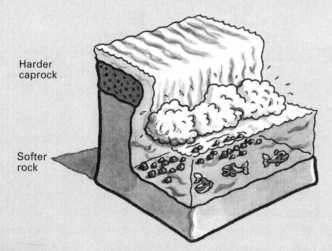

Harder caprock

Softer rock

A waterfall is formed where a riverbed suddenly plunges down to a lower level. Waterfalls are created when a layer of softer rock has been worn away through erosion, while a hard layer of caprock remains at the top of the waterfall.

World's Highest Waterfalls

The Angel River in Venezuela, South America, leaps over a cliff to the riverbed below, to create the highest waterfall on Earth. The Angel Falls plunge 3,212 feet (979 m) from the top of the Guiana highlands. The amazing falls are named after the American pilot James Angel, who was the first person to see them from the air, in 1935.

Many mountain waterfalls appear in high, rocky places that are difficult to visit. Fortunately, Niagara Falls is very easy to visit. Another exception is Victoria Falls, a beautiful mountain waterfall in Africa. This spectacular waterfall drops 354 feet (108 m) into a narrow space at the valley bottom, called the "Boiling Pot." There, the water churns and roars, making its way out of a small channel to continue the river's course. Victoria Falls are on the Zimbabwe-Zambia border in south central Africa. They were discovered in 1855 by the British explorer, David Livingstone, who named them for Queen Victoria.

WATER AT WORK

Construct a waterwheel, and discover how falling water can make a simple machine work.

What You Need:
- Half-gallon (1.9-liter) milk carton (empty and clean)

- Scissors

- Pencil

- A 6-inch (15.2 centimeter[cm]) piece of string

- Finger ring

- Measuring cup

- Water

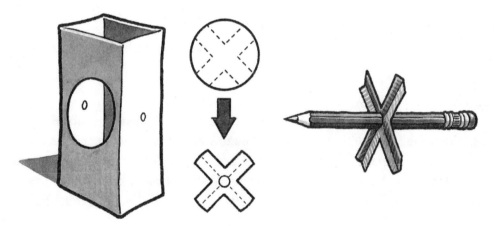

What to Do:
1. Open up the top of the milk carton completely.
2. Cut a 3-inch (7.6 cm) circle out of one side of the milk carton.
3. Cut four evenly spaced triangles around the edge of the circle, stopping about $\frac{1}{2}$ inch (1.3 cm) from the center of the circle.
4. Fold each quarter section of the remaining wheel in half down the middle.
5. Push the pencil through the center of the wheel.

continued

6. Carefully take the pencil out of the wheel without making the hole larger. When you reinsert the pencil later, you will want it to be snug.

7. Push the pencil through the side of the milk carton, next to the side in which you cut the hole. Twist the pencil back and forth a few times so that it can easily twist in the hole.

8. Place the wheel *inside* the carton and push the pencil through the wheel. Keep pushing the pencil until it pokes through the other side of the carton. Twist at this end, too, so that the pencil twists easily in the hole. Leave most of the pencil sticking out the other end.

9. Tie the string to the eraser end of the pencil. Make sure it is tight and won't slip.

10. Tie the ring to the other end of the string.

11. Pour water from the measuring cup into the carton from the top, aiming the stream at the wheel.

What Happens and Why:

The water hits the flat surfaces of the wheel and makes it turn. The wheel makes the pencil turn, and the string begins to wrap around the pencil. As the string becomes shorter, the ring moves upward. The power of the water drives a machine that does the work of lifting the ring. Waterwheels in rivers have been used for thousands of years to set many different types of machines in motion.

a cliff 180 feet (55 m) high. The water slipped over an edge 1,100 feet (330 m) long. It was pretty, but it wasn't as dramatic as I had expected. Then we drove over to the Canadian side of the falls. The loud roar of falling water got louder . . . and *louder* . . . and LOUDER.

e parked the car and walked over to the viewing area. Wow! Now *this*, I thought, is a natural wonder! My wife, two children, and I stood speechless as we watched the massive volume of water drop over a giant horseshoe-shaped cliff. Although the Canadian Horseshoe Falls are not quite as tall as the American Falls, their cliff edge is 2,500 feet (750 m) long. Ninety percent of the water flowing down Niagara Falls drops over the Canadian side. An amazing 3 billion gallons (11 billion liters [l]) per hour drops to the deep gorge below the Horseshoe Falls. Spray shoots up as the water hits the rocky side of the cliff and bounces off the river below. Sun reflecting off the drops of water in the air create small rainbows, and the explosive power of billions of gallons of water on the run sounds like thunder.

3

Caves
WONDERS IN THE DARK

One evening, teenage cowboy Jim White was riding his horse a few miles from the 4X Ranch in New Mexico where he worked. He noticed a swirl of dark smoke curling up into the sky above the foothills of the Guadalupe Mountains. What could be burning in the sandy desert? Curious, Jim rode toward the smoke, which grew darker and thicker as he got nearer. A strange rushing sound filled the air. After galloping up to the foothills, his horse stopped near the edge of a large black pit in the ground. The smoke wasn't smoke at all—it was **alive!** Streaming out of the hole were thousands of bats!

Jim had discovered the entryway into a giant bat cave, just when the furry mammals were speeding out into the night to feed on insects. It took three hours for all the bats to leave the cave. If this hole led to the home of so many bats, Jim knew it must be a very big place.

When the last bat had flown out, Jim found some lightweight sticks, set them on fire, and threw them down the hole. The light was not strong enough to reveal anything, though Jim couldn't wait to see what was down there in the dark. He made a ladder out of some sticks and rope, and he tied one end to a rock. Scared and shaking, he lowered himself down and then tried to find little ledges for his feet along the wall. Finally, he lowered himself down to a big ledge. Lighting up some sticks as a torch, he looked around him. Towering from the floor far below him and hanging from the ceiling were the most amazing things Jim had ever seen—shiny columns and what looked like giant icicles, huge frozen waterfalls, and solid drapes that seemed to float along the walls.

On that evening in 1901, Jim White discovered what are now called "Carlsbad Caverns" in southeastern New Mexico. He ended up spending the rest of his life exploring and working in the caverns, as well as sharing their beauty with as many people as possible. A **cave** is a natural opening into the side of a hill or a cliff, or a large hole underground. A very large cave is a **cavern.**

Solution Caves

Carlsbad Caverns are one example of **solution caves** or **limestone caves.** Over millions of years, the action of water ꙅꭼꭼᖘꙕꞑᎶ through rock creates a solution cave. Most solution caves occur in rock called "limestone," but they can also form in marble, dolomite, and gypsum rock.

How a Solution Cave Is Formed

The process that produces solution caves is as great a wonder as the magical, complex, and beautifully decorated solution caves themselves. When standing in a solution cave, feeling tiny next to the huge structures on the ceiling, floor, and walls, it's almost impossible to imagine that everything was formed by water . . . drop by drop. The birth of a solution cave begins with rain:

1. As rainwater falls through the air and seeps into the ground, it collects carbon dioxide (a gas that is a mixture of carbon and oxygen). When water mixes with carbon dioxide, it makes a weak acid called "carbonic acid."
2. The watery carbonic-acid solution then passes into the soil and through cracks in limestone rock. When **calcite** (the main mineral in limestone) is exposed to the carbonic acid, it breaks up and dissolves into the watery carbonic-acid solution.
3. The watery solution eats away at the limestone, creating holes in the rock. More and more holes open, creating a **chamber,** a larger space. The watery solution then flows between chambers in a **cave passage,** a narrow tunnel.

> To remember the difference between a stalactite and a stalagmite, think: stalactites hold "tite" (as they hang).

The Awesome Inner World of Solution Caves

The many different types of structures inside a solution cave are **speleothems** (from the Greek word *spelaion*, which means "cave," and *thema*, which means "deposit"). The most common speleothems are stalactites and stalagmites. Anyone who's ever heard of a cave (unless they've been living in one all their lives) has heard of these two objects: a **stalactite** hangs like an **icicle** from the ceiling, and a **stalagmite** grows up from the ground.

Stalactites form as drops of water seep through the cave ceiling. When a drop of water reaches the surface and hangs from the ceiling, it loses its carbon dioxide. Without the carbon dioxide, the water no longer carries carbonic acid. This allows the calcite to separate from the water and become solid rock again. Calcite that has emerged from a drop of water is **dripstone.**

Stalactites grow about 1 inch (2.54 cm) every 100 years.

Drop by drop, the dripstone forms ring upon ring, extending down toward the ground. Eventually, the rings grow into a delicate hollow tube that seldom grows longer than 1 yard (0.91m). This fragile tube, as thick as a drop of water, is a **soda straw stalactite.** A large cone-shaped stalactite starts out as a soda straw. When enough water drips into the tube to fill it up and spill over the top, the dripstone then gathers on the outside of the tube. The dripstone layers are thickest near the ceiling and taper off at the bottom.

Stalagmites form on the ground as water drips from the overhanging stalactites, leaving rings of dripstone to build up in layers. When a stalagmite grows tall enough to meet an overhead stalactite, they join together to make a **column.**

Any visit to a cave will reveal that dripstone creates many more forms than just stalactites, stalagmites, and columns. Water trickling down the slope of the ceiling forms into delicate folds as **curtain** or **drapery** speleothems. Rippling sheets of stone called "flowstone" are created by flows of dripstone down a wall or onto the floor. A **helictite** is a thin, twisting structure that sprouts from the ceiling or wall like **spaghetti**. Its odd shape results from water that is dripping so slowly that changes in the air affect the chemical structure of the calcite. A **rimstone** dam forms a raised rim around the edge of a pool on the cave floor, jutting up from the ground like a fence. Dripstone that falls on and surrounds a piece of sand forms a **cave pearl.**

The most common color of cave structures is some shade of tan, but elements such as iron and magnesium, found in the water and the rock, may add delicate color. Spelunkers shine their flashlights onto some mild rose shades on a flowing drape or some green and purple hues on the shiny layers of a majestic stalagmite.

A limestone cave contains many amazing structures, each formed by dripstone, one drop at a time.

Spelunking, Anyone?

The Latin word for cave is *spelunca*. A cave explorer is a **spelunker,** and to explore a cave is to go *spelunking*. A scientist who studies caves is a **speleologist.**

The Coolest Caverns

Carlsbad Caverns

When young Jim White began exploring the caves beneath the Guadalupe Mountains, he entered a world that had begun forming 60 million years ago, when the mountain range itself

GROW A STALACTITE!

Using a mixture of water and soda, you can grow a small stalactite in just a few days.

What You Need:
- Two pickle jars
- Washing soda
- Thick wool yarn
- Two paper clips
- Saucer
- Spoon

What to Do:
1. Fill each jar with very warm water.
2. Add washing soda to each jar, stirring and adding more until the soda can no longer dissolve in the water.
3. Cut about a 15 inch (38 cm) length of wool yarn.
4. Attach a paper clip to each end of the wool yarn.
5. Place the saucer between the two jars.
6. Lower each end of the string into a jar so that the string is hanging over the saucer.
7. Leave the jars undisturbed for two to three days.

What Happens and Why:
The wool yarn absorbs the water-soda solution from each jar. As the dripping water *evaporates,* the soda is left behind as a solid and clumps into a stalactite. Drops of water that fall into the dish may also build a small stalagmite. In the same way, calcite separates from water inside a cave to form dripstone stalactites, stalagmites, and other objects.

Please Don't Touch!

Vistors to caves and spelunkers are taught to keep their hands away from stalagmites and other cave structures. One touch can destroy one year of drip-by-drip growth!

sprang up. With each rainfall, water flowed into the cracks of the rock to the deeper rocks below the ground. As the passageways grew, the water traveled more quickly and carved through the rock with more force. When the water flows into a layer of salt or gypsum rock, the erosion process is faster because these kinds of rock dissolve more easily than limestone does. When rainfall is heavy, an underground stream may form. Each stream works its way to the lowest area it can find and then slowly washes away the underlying rock.

Carlsbad Caverns are an underground network of passages, caves, and caverns 14.9 miles (24 km) long. The bat cave that drew Jim White to the place is at the top level of the caverns, about 200 feet (61 m) below the surface, and is not open to the public. Not only is it full of bats, which might not appeal to every visitor, but it's also full of bat dung, or *guano*, which may be the worst-smelling stuff on Earth! Guano is an excellent fertilizer for crops and, for many years, Jim White supervised a guano-mining business in the caverns. The big bucket used to lower miners into the bat cave became the first elevator to bring a visitor into the caverns. This metal bucket is on display at the Carlsbad Caverns today.

The main corridor leading from the cave entrance sweeps down into the second level of the caverns, which lies 750 feet (229 m) below the surface. The third level reaches more than 1,000 feet (305 m) below ground. The most astonishing spectacle in the caverns is found in the second level, the Big Room, the largest cavern in the United States. What else could you call a cavern that covers *14 acres* (5.6 hectares)? With stalactites of every size pointing down from the ceiling, this giant cavern is 1,800 feet (549 m) long, up to 1,100 feet (335 m) wide, with a ceiling 225 feet (69 m) high. The floor is a forest of stone objects, including groups of towering stalagmites with names such as the Totem Poles, the Twin Domes, and the Giant Dome.

The World's Rarest Speleothem

In the caves of the Gunung Mulu region of Borneo, an island northwest of Australia, a bizarre speleothem grows that is not found anywhere else in the world. The **showerhead** sprouts from the ceiling of a cave, narrow at the base and spreading out like, well, like a showerhead! The showerheads of Borneo grow to about 1.6 feet (0.5 m) long and 3.3 feet (1 m) wide.

Although Carlsbad Caverns is not the longest cave system in the country (Mammoth Cave in Kentucky is the longest), the size of the Big Room and the depth of the caverns make it the *largest* cave in the United States. In fact, no one knows exactly how deep its caverns are because they have not yet been completely explored.

Today, a large spring about 10 miles (16 km) away from the caverns flows out to the earth's surface. This water from underground contains about one *teaspoon* of solid matter to every gallon (3.8 l) of water, which means that it carries about 30,000 tons (27,300 metric tons) of limestone, salt, and gypsum out of the ground every year. Deep within Carlsbad Caverns, nature is still at work carving dark spaces into the ancient stone.

Mammoth Cave

About 260 million years ago, the land that became Kentucky was part of an area of the continent covered by a shallow sea. The seafloor slowly began to lift up, pushed from below by movements within the *mantle*, the layer of Earth containing melted rock. The rising land made the sea drain away, leaving the seabed exposed to the air and *sun*. The mud, sand, and other particles of the seabed hardened into layers of three kinds of rock: sandstone, shale, and limestone. With every rainfall, water seeped through the rock and began carving holes, passages, and caves. After millions of years, the water created the longest cave system in the world, 169 miles (272 km) of underground passages and caves now known as "Mammoth Cave."

Unlike Carlsbad Caverns, Mammoth Cave is not famous for its huge caverns or large variety of stalactites and stalagmites. What makes Mammoth Cave special are its unusual formations, the length of its passages, and

Weird Cave Creatures

The deep, dark rivers of Mammoth Cave are home to fish that have no eyes. Because there is no light deep within the cave, the fish rely on their senses of touch, smell, and taste, rather than sight. These famous eyeless fish grow no bigger than 3 to 4 inches (8 to 10 cm) in length.

These fish appear to be white because they have no pigments (coloring) in their skin or their scales. Pigment protects the skin from harmful rays of the sun. Creatures that live in complete darkness, however, do not develop skin pigments because they do not need this protection.

Another river creature found in deep caves is the blind crawfish, which is so translucent you can almost see right through it. Cave crickets are also translucent, unlike their dark, shiny cousins up on the surface. *Cave beetles,* small bugs found in deep caves, are blind.

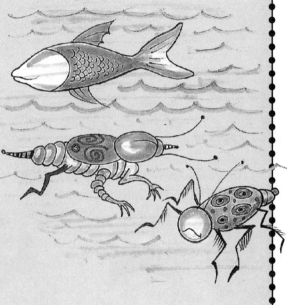

its rivers. The cave's most breathtaking speleothems include a huge waterfall-shaped formation called "Niagara Falls," 50 feet (15 m) wide and 75 feet (23 m) high! Visitors to the cave can take a boat ride, 350 feet (107 m) underground, on the Echo River. This **winding river** is from 20 to 60 feet (6 to 18 m) wide and from 5 to 25 feet (1.5 to 8 m) deep. The river got its name from the mysterious sounds heard along its course. The splash of the water against the cave, the sound of a human voice, the vibrations of a tiny stalactite that is moved by a current of air—each sound bounces against the cavern walls and is heard in a series of echoes.

The Deepest Cave in the United States

In Utah, Neff Canyon extends 1,189 feet (362 m) below the surface, the deepest cave explored in the United States. The second deepest cave is part of Carlsbad Caverns, where the lowest known point is 1,022 feet (312 m) below the cave entrance.

The Cave of the Winds

In the Black Hills of South Dakota, a limestone cave called "Wind Cave" is one of the native Sioux's most sacred places. According to the Sioux tradition, buffalo first came from this cave where the wind always blew. This cave's opening often whistles with high wind. The wind is caused by changes in air pressure. Air, or wind, always moves from an area of high pressure to one of low pressure. When the air pressure outside the cave is high, the wind rushes into the cave. When the air pressure drops, such as before a storm, the air rushes out. Wind Cave is now a national park covering nearly 30,000 acres (12,000 hectares).

Earth's Own Twilight Zone: The Sections of a Cave

Explorers and researchers have named different sections of caves that extend down into the earth. The area starting from the mouth of the cave and going as far inside as daylight can be seen is the **twilight zone.** Animals such as birds, snakes, mice, and skunks live in the twilight zone. In the summer, the temperature in the twilight zone is cooler than the temperature outside, and in winter, it is slightly warmer. The next section is the **variable temperature zone,** which changes somewhat in temperature, but not as much as the twilight zone does. Living in the darkness of this part of a cave are bats, cave crickets, salamanders, and growing things such as mushrooms, mold, and other fungi.

The deepest, darkest part of a cave is called the **constant temperature zone,** in which the air and water have a constant temperature of 56° Fahrenheit (13° Celsius). These pitch-black areas of famous caves such as Carlsbad Caverns and Mammoth Cave have been set up with electricity to provide light for visitors. The air feels moist and smells moldy in the constant temperature zone.

Other Amazing Caves

Although solution caves are the most common type of caves found on Earth, caves are created in other ways, too. Other types of caves include sea caves, lava caves, and glacier caves.

A sea cave on the island of Kayaking Palau in Micronesia was used as a seaplane hangar by the Japanese during World War II.

Sea Caves

Wherever the ocean pounds away at a rocky shore, **sea caves** may be hollowed out of the rock. On Sandwick Island, one of the Orkney Islands in the North Sea north of Scotland, lies a sea cave named Hole O'Rowe. Sand, pebbles, and water have crashed into the cliff for millions of years, forming a deep hole. The Channel Islands off the coast of southern California are dotted with sea caves. When the sea is calm, visitors paddle in and out of the cave arches in small boats called "kayaks." When the waves are rough, kayaking is too dangerous, because the waters act like a huge washing machine that would crash a boat against the walls of the caves.

The waves that *erode* (break down) the side of a cliff create tremendous air pressure in the cracks of the rock. When air is forced through the cracks, it pushes the rock apart. Each time a wave hits the rock, air and water from the cave below crash through cracks to the outside. This type of opening in a cliff is a **blowhole.**

The largest sea caves in the world are found along the Oregon coast of the United States. Sea Lion Caves were formed 25 million years ago and cut into giant cliffs as high as 12-story buildings. One of the country's true natural wonders, Sea Lion Caves are home to wild sea lions. Giant male sea lions, weighing up to 2,000 pounds (900 kilograms [kg]), golden-colored female sea lions, and shiny black sea lion pups lie on the rock ledges outside the caves and sun themselves.

Lava Caves

The eruption of a volcano can create mysterious hidden spaces after the *lava* (melted rock) has cooled. When lava flows down the side of the mountain, the outer surface cools, while the hot lava beneath the surface keeps moving along, creating a lava tube. When all the lava has drained away from inside the lava tube, hollow spaces remain. These spaces, **lava caves,** are found in many parts of the world where volcanoes have been active.

In northeastern China, a lava cave lies in a cliff surrounding beautiful Jingbo Lake. On the island of Kauai in Hawaii, Waikapala's Wet Cave was formed by a lava flow. Africa's Chyulu Mountains in Kenya are home to lava caves formed from cooled lava flows. Kenyans call this area of lava flows "Shetani," which means "devil" in the Swahili language.

In Italy, from 1991 to 1993, lava eruptions of Mount Etna created a lava cave, which was not explored until 1994. This lava cave is 2,854 feet (870 m) long and 318 feet (97 m) deep. Explorers had to wait a year after the last eruption in 1993 because the air inside the lava tube was too hot to enter before then. In fact, some other lava caves from the same eruption, are *still* too hot to explore!

Glacier Caves

A **glacier** is a huge sheet of ice found in polar regions and on mountains, formed by many layers of snow that do not melt because of freezing temperatures. (We dig into the whole story of glaciers in Chapter 6.) Beneath some glaciers lie open spaces that have been formed by water. Because glaciers weigh many tons, the pressure of the heavy glacier melts the very bottom of the ice sheet into *meltwater* (melted ice water). Some of this meltwater seeps into cracks in the glacier and drains off as a stream. The moving action of the stream then cuts through the ice, carving out a space that grows into a cave.

Caves in Europe: The World's First Art Galleries

Near the end of the Paleolithic era of Earth's history, from about 30,000 years to 10,000 years ago, cave-dwelling people created beautiful drawings on the walls inside their cave homes. The oldest paintings in the world are found in a cave at Vogelherd, in West Germany. These pictures, painted by the light of fires and torches, are believed to be more than 30,000 years old. The most famous caves containing prehistoric art are found in southern France and northwestern Spain, in limestone caves in and around the Pyrenees Mountains.

Cave artists used substances containing iron and manganese to make their paints. Iron created reds and yellows, and manganese was used for dark browns and black. The iron and the manganese were ground into a powder and added to a liquid, made of either water or melted animal fat. Apparently, before the pictures were painted, they were sketched in charcoal. The paint was applied with brushes made of sticks or hair, or with soft pads made of moss or animal skin. Instead of paintings, some cave artists used a sharp stick or stone to carve a picture into the rock, creating a sculpture within the wall.

Cave drawings portray the animals that lived during those times, including red deer, reindeer, mammoths, bison, horses, and wild cattle. A few caves in eastern Spain also contain pictures of people, but most cave art is devoted to animals.

24

Mountains

SCALING THE HEIGHTS

For many years, men and women who love nature and enjoy challenging themselves have climbed mountains for sport. High above the clouds, the climber is alone with the wind, the rock, and nearby climbing companions. Climbing takes physical strength and great concentration. (I think it sounds like a great sport, but I haven't tried it yet—the highest I've climbed up is a steep hill in San Francisco!)

Modern equipment has increased the safety of mountain climbing, but crumbling icy rock faces, flat cliffs, and sudden weather changes have taken the lives of many climbers.

Nearly 150 people have died trying to climb Mount Everest, the tallest mountain in the world, including 8 people who perished in May of 1996, when a massive storm hit the mountain.

A Mountain Mystery

The biggest unsolved mystery in *mountaineering* (the sport of climbing mountains) involves an attempt to reach the *summit* (highest point) of Mount Everest (29,028 ft.), the top of the world, in June of 1924. Two British climbers, George Mallory and Andrew Irvine, had reached higher than anyone else on the peak. Just 800 feet (244 m) from the top, they began their final climb. At this point, they were already more than 5 miles (8 km) above sea level. Noel Odell, a member of the expedition, was exploring the mountain thousands of feet below. When the clouds cleared away for a few moments that afternoon, Odell looked up and saw two tiny black spots moving toward the top. He was thrilled to see his friends so close to the summit of the mountain. "Then," Odell wrote, "the whole fascinating vision vanished, enveloped in cloud once more." The clouds covered Mallory and Irvine from view for the last time. They were never seen again.

Odell and the rest of the group searched for the pair but never found them. Did one or both of the lost climbers make it to the top before they died, becoming the first in the world to do so? How did they vanish? Did they slip and fall, were they covered by an avalanche, or did they run out of oxygen? Climbers hunted for signs of Mallory and Irvine during four expeditions in the 1930s and discovered only one clue: an ice ax lying on a ridge.

Making Mountain History

Twenty-nine years after Mallory and Irvine vanished from Mount Everest, two climbers successfully reached the mountain's summit and became the most famous mountain explorers in the world. Edmund Hillary, a beekeeper from New Zealand, reached the top with Tenzing Norkay, a Sherpa guide from Nepal. The morning of May 29, 1953, Hillary and Norkay climbed out of their tent to begin the final stretch of their climb to the top of Everest. Their first challenge was to move along a sharp, narrow *crest* (edge) of the mountain. On

The Sherpa people live in the Himalayas and have worked for hundreds of years as traders carrying goods across the mountains. Their mountaineering skills and strength have earned Sherpa people the name "Tigers of the Snow."

Mountaineering Gear

One of the greatest problems in climbing high mountains is lack of oxygen. The air in high levels of the atmosphere contains less oxygen than does the air near sea level. Mountain climbers carry tanks of oxygen to help them breathe.

Most of the climber's face is covered with an oxygen mask and snow goggles. Climbers also carry ice axes with which they cut steps into the ice and snow. Axes can also save climbers' lives by stopping them from falling if they slip on the ice or snow. Mountain climbers also wear boots fitted with steel spikes called "crampons," which bite like claws into the ice. Another very important piece of safety equipment is the climber's rope. Tied around the waist, the rope is anchored to rock or ice with a metal clip called a "karabiner."

Mountain climbing in high peaks requires special equipment.

Another Famous Hillary

Hillary Rodham Clinton, wife of President Bill (William Jefferson) Clinton, was named after explorer Edmund Hillary. Her mother read an article about Edmund Hillary before her daughter was born on October 26, 1947, and admired the heroic explorer (six years before he made his most famous climb of all).

both sides, the crest dropped straight down. Like tightrope walkers without a net, they slowly made their way up the crest to a slope of crumbling snow. Just one slip would have caused either man to fall down a side of the mountain five times higher than the highest skyscraper in the world. Halfway up the slope, the snowy surface broke beneath Hillary's feet. He slid a few feet, but stopped himself by jabbing his ax into the hard snow and hanging on until he could get his footing. The two climbers then continued up the slope and safely made it to the next obstacle: another razor-sharp ridge to cross.

This tightrope act was even more dangerous than the last. Jutting up like teeth of a saw, the rocky edge led down to a vast wall of bare rock on the left. On the right, wind had piled up huge towers of snow weighing hundreds of tons. These leaning white towers, which mountain climbers call "cornices," could split away from the rock at any time, crashing to the valley far below. The only way to get to the top was to walk across those cornices.

Hillary and Norkay checked their oxygen tanks. They had enough left for four and one-half hours of climbing. If they could reach the top in two and one-half hours, they'd have enough oxygen to get back to base camp. That meant that they must reach the top by 11:30 that morning or they would have to turn back.

To avoid stepping over the least-safe-looking cornices, Hillary and Norkay moved to the left. They cut steps into the side of the rock edge and clung to handholds cut in the snow, moving along footholds on the rock. After safely clearing the narrowest part of the crest, they moved slowly up the hard snow. Hillary noticed that his partner was falling behind. He stopped to check Norkay's oxygen tubes and discovered that one tube was blocked with ice. Hillary quickly cleared it away, and Norkay could breathe again. They would both need every ounce of oxygen for the obstacle to come.

After an hour of climbing, they came to a sudden stop at a wall of rock rising 40 feet (12 m) straight up. The smooth face of the rock wall offered nothing to hold onto. Would they have to turn back? By sliding toward an overhang of frozen snow that covered part of the wall, Hillary found a large crack. The only way up was to climb the crack.

With nowhere to tie a safety rope, Hillary began inching his way up the wall next to the layer of frozen snow. He pressed his body into the crack and stuck the steel spikes of his shoes into the snow. Pulling himself up, he stuck his shoes in at a higher spot in the snow. Every move demanded all of Hillary's energy. He felt his strength failing. Looking down at Norkay, Hillary thought of all the work his Sherpa friend and the rest of the members of the *expedition* had done to get them this far. Hillary found the courage to drive himself upward. When he reached the flat top of the wall, he fell to the ground and caught his breath. Then it was Norkay's turn. Hillary helped Norkay scale the wall by pulling on the rope that connected them.

After the hours of exhausting work, it was nearly 11:30. They had one more minute before they would have to turn back. Wearily raising his head above a clump of snow, Hillary pulled himself up and looked around. He couldn't believe his eyes. As he moved his head to survey the scene, Hillary was looking *down*. He was on the very top! After Hillary called Norkay to his side, the two climbers stood together on the highest spot on Earth!

Hillary quickly took some photographs, which would appear in newspapers all over the world. Battling freezing temperatures, icy winds, and the most dangerous surfaces on Earth, Edmund Hillary and Tenzing Norkay pulled all of their courage and strength together to make history.

The first people to climb to the peak of Mount Everest were Edmund Hillary of New Zealand and Tenzing Norkay of Nepal in 1953. Looking out from the highest point in the world, Norkay said in the Sherpa language, "Thuji chey, Chomolungma," which means "I am grateful, Goddess Mother of the World."

Why They Climb

James W. Whittaker, first American to climb Mount Everest: "I have such a strong love of nature that I think that being in nature in the mountains or at sea or in the wilds is the most true and real experience a human being can have."

Richard D. Bass, first person to climb the highest mountain on each of the seven continents: "Whatever confidence I have comes from striving . . . and I'm not going to sit back in my rocking chair and take it easy."

Naoe Sakashita, leader of a Japanese team to the top of the second tallest mountain in the world, K2:

"Under the dangerous conditions, I found something. I found myself under the severe conditions. Maybe I can express myself through climbing. I am different from any other person."

Royal Robbins, American climber and author: "The important thing is to concentrate on doing the best you can rather than on what you are trying to achieve . . . thinking about what you are doing at the moment and doing it as well as you can."

Arlene Blum, leader of the first American ascent of Annapurna: "It's an ultimate challenge. You get to use all of your skills—physical, mental, and spiritual—and focus on one goal. I do like to dream something up and make it happen."

Mountain Building

What caused Mount Everest to rise up more than 5 miles (8 km) above the surface of Earth? Most mountains on Earth were formed in one of four ways, each taking place over long periods of time. These processes form four basic types of mountains: (1) volcanic mountains, (2) fold mountains, (3) fault-block mountains, and (4) dome mountains.

Volcanic Mountains

Volcanic mountains, such as Japan's Mount Fuji and Hawaii's Mauna Kea, form when *molten* (melted) rock from deep inside Earth erupts to the surface. The molten rock piles up and hardens to form a mountain. Even though Mount Everest is the tallest peak above sea level, Mauna Kea is technically the tallest

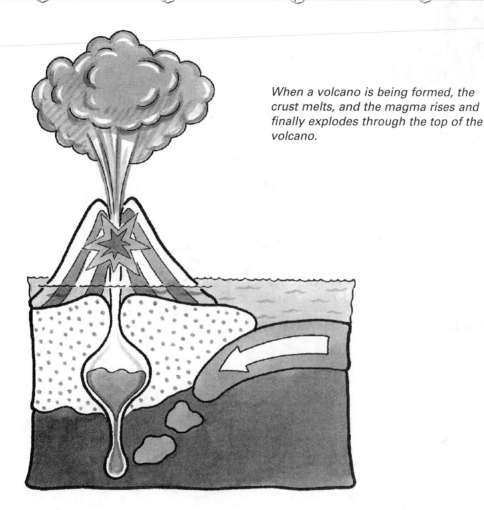

When a volcano is being formed, the crust melts, and the magma rises and finally explodes through the top of the volcano.

mountain on Earth. From its base at the bottom of the sea to its peak, Mauna Kea is 33,476 feet (10,043 m) high.

The Andes Mountains, which stretch about 4,500 miles (7,200 km) along the west coast of South America, were formed by volcanic eruptions over the past 65 million years. This range is part of a zone of volcanic activity that forms a circular pattern around the Pacific Ocean, called the "Ring of Fire."

One of the world's most active volcanoes is Popocatepetl in Mexico. Located about 43 miles (70 km) southeast of Mexico City, Popo is the fifth tallest mountain in the world and is considered by many to be one of Earth's natural wonders. After 50 years of quiet, Popo blasted back into action in December 1994. The mountain rises 17,925 feet (5,465 km) above sea level and has erupted more than 15 times since Spanish explorers arrived in Mexico in 1519. Since the late 1994 eruption, *ash* (bits of melted rock that have

BUILD YOUR OWN ERUPTING VOLCANO!

What You Need:
- Funnel

- A 16-ounce plastic soda bottle

- Baking soda

- Smaller plastic bottle

- Vinegar

- Red food coloring

- Cake pan or baking dish

- Soil and sand

What to Do:
1. Place the funnel in the mouth of the soda bottle, and pour in baking soda until the bottle is half full.
2. Fill the smaller bottle about half full of vinegar.
3. Add about 6 drops of food coloring to the vinegar.
4. Stand the soda bottle in the center of the pan, and pile soil and sand around it in the shape of a mountain. The mouth of the soda bottle should be showing on top, with the funnel resting in it.
5. Quickly pour the red vinegar into the soda bottle through the funnel.

What Happens and Why:
The vinegar reacts with the baking soda to form carbon-dioxide gas. The gas expands out of the bottle, just as the gases in magma cause it to erupt from a volcano. The red "lava" in this activity was carried to the surface through the opening in the soda bottle.

Popocatepetl News Flash

As I write this chapter, hundreds of thousands of people are being evacuated from towns near Popocatepetl. Just yesterday, on June 30, 1997, the volcano had its biggest eruption since 1925, sending ash 7.5 miles (12 km) into the air and spurting fountains of lava 1,500 feet (450 m) high. For the first time in 70 years, ash from the volcano has fallen on Mexico City.

What's going on with Popocatepetl right now? Check it out on one of my favorite websites, "Volcano World" (http://volcano.und.nodak.edu/vw.html).

Paricutín—Mountain in a Cornfield

On February 20, 1943, smoke was discovered coming out of a small crack in the ground in a Mexican cornfield. The field was near the village of Paricutín, about 200 miles (320 km) west of Mexico City. That night, the crack was blown open in an eruption that sent thousands of tons of lava and ash into the air. In one week, the lava and fallen ash had formed a cone about 450 feet (140 m) high. The people who lived in the villages of Paricutín and nearby San Juan Parangaricútir were evacuated before both villages became completely buried in ash.

Volcanologists (scientists who study volcanoes) arrived on the scene to watch, for the first time, the birth of a volcano from first blast to towering mountain. By the eighth week, the volcano reached a height of about 1,000 feet (300 m). The mountain rumbled on for nine years and last erupted in 1952. Paricutín is the youngest volcano in the Western Hemisphere and now stands 1,345 feet (410 m) from base to summit. The volcano's sudden appearance and rapid growth makes Paricutín one of the world's natural wonders.

cooled into flakes) has continued to pour out of the top of the volcano. In October 1996, Popo erupted with an ash column rising about 27,000 feet (9,000 m) above the top of the volcano. With more than 20 million people living near Popocatepetl, scientists are watching the volcano very closely to warn people of dangerous eruptions.

Ayers Rock: Australian Wonder

An awesome natural wonder is Ayers Rock, in the middle of Australia. This rock is left over from mountains that were built about 550 million years ago. About 2 miles (3.1 km) long and 1.2 miles (2 km) wide, the gigantic red rock reaches 1,132 feet (345 m) above a dry, flat plain. Ayers is a recycled mountain. The original mountain range was worn down to rubble through millions of years of erosion. The rocky rubble was then pressed into a layer of rock when the sea covered the area. About 400 million years ago, Earth movements pushed up some of this rock layer above sea level. After the sea receded, the rock was exposed to erosion once again. Softer layers of rock that once surrounded Ayers have disappeared through erosion, leaving this hard, quartz-rich, giant rock to stand alone on the plain.

Fold Mountains

Fold mountains, such as the Alps in Europe, are formed by tremendous forces inside Earth. The *crust* (outer layer) of Earth is made of several rocky *plates* (large, movable segments of Earth's crust). The continents lie on top of these plates. Like giant leaves floating on a huge lake, Earth's plates float on a layer of partly

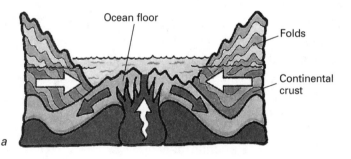

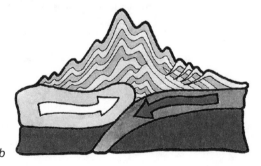

Mountains are built from the collision of two plates.

(a) As two continents move toward each other over millions of years, they squeeze the ocean floor that separates them. As the oceanic crust is crushed and pushed deep into the earth, magma is created. The magma rises near the edges of each continent, pushing up the continental crust.

(b) As the plates continue to move together, the crust lifts, crumples, and folds, building a mountain range.

Major Peaks

	35,000 ft.
	30,000 ft.
	25,000 ft.
	20,000 ft.
	15,000 ft.
	10,000 ft.
	5,000 ft.
	0 ft.

| Everest (Asia) 29,028 ft | Aconcagua (South America) 22,831 ft | McKinley (North America) 20,320 ft | Kilimanjaro (Africa) 19,340 ft | Elbrus (Europe) 18,510 ft | Vison Massif (Antartica) 16,066 ft | Kosciusko (Australia) 7,310 ft |

How do the world's tallest mountains stack up against one another? Here is the height of the highest peak on each continent.

The Highest and Lowest Points on Earth

Highest: Top of Mount Everest, 29,028 feet (8,848 m) above sea level.

Lowest: Bottom of the Marianas Trench in the Pacific Ocean, 36,198 feet (10,860 m) below the ocean floor.

melted rock, called the "mantle." The constantly moving plates have crashed into one another and broken apart several times in Earth's history.

When two edges of a plate collide, they crumple up and fold along the line where they meet. The stretch of folded, twisted, heaped-up rock between the two plates are *fold mountains*. The Himalayas are fold mountains, created as the plate beneath India collides with the plate beneath Tibet and China. The long seam where these plates meet is still squeezing together today, so the Himalayas are continuing to rise, with Mount Everest growing about 0.4 inches

(1 cm) taller every year. More than 40 of the tallest mountains in the world are found in the Himalayas.

Fault-Block Mountains

Fault-block mountains form when huge blocks of Earth are pushed up along a crack in the ground called a "fault." The Harz Mountains in Germany and the Teton Range in Wyoming were built in this way. A piece of Earth's crust slides up along the fault and rises above the surface to form a mountain.

Dome Mountains

ome mountains, such as the Black Hills of South Dakota, are also created by a push from deep within Earth. The movement of the mantle sometimes causes a section of crust to rise into a huge bulge or dome. Exposed to wind and rain, the softer, outer layer of the dome wears away. This erosion exposes the harder layers of rock, which do not wear down as quickly. Another example of dome mountains are the Adirondack Mountains of New York State.

A close-up look at the powerful forces that build mountains can be found in *Shake, Rattle, and Roll*, the second book in my World of Wonders series.

Mountain Creatures

Several different types of animals live on mountain slopes. The most common mountain dwellers are wild sheep and goats that have developed great balance and fancy footwork. These animals run and play along steep, rocky mountainsides without slipping. The mountains of central Asia are home to a huge type of sheep called *Ovis poli*, which stand 4 feet (4.9 m) high and weigh up to 600 pounds (270 kg). Big mountain-dwelling sheep in other parts of the world include the argali of Tibet and the bighorn sheep of North America.

Many varieties of large cats also live in the mountains of the world. The brown mountain lion, or puma, lives in the mountains of North and South America. The snow leopard of the Himalayas is light gray with dark spots, and travels over the snow on large, broad paws. One of the largest members of the cat family, the Siberian tiger, also lives in the mountains of Asia. There are three large *preserves* (protected areas) for tigers in the mountain regions of eastern Russia.

The giant panda lives in the mountains of central China, where it spends about 75 percent of its day eating bamboo. This black-and-white bearlike animal stands up to 4.5 feet (1.4 m) tall and weighs up to 350 pounds (158 kg). Grizzly bears, some of the biggest bears in the world, are found in the mountain forests of North America, Europe, and Asia. These big meat eaters can grow up to 8 feet (2.4 m) tall and weigh up to 500 pounds (225 kg). Grizzly bears eat plants and meat, including deer and moose.

Long-haired yaks, members of the cattle family, are used to carry heavy loads in the mountains of Tibet. The yak has a very thick coat that protects it from the cold temperatures and icy winds of the mountains.

Some people have told tales of a mysterious creature—half-man, half-ape—who lives in the Himalaya Mountains. The abominable snowman, which the Sherpa people call "Yeti," is supposed to be covered with brownish fur and to leave footprints 16 inches (41 cm)

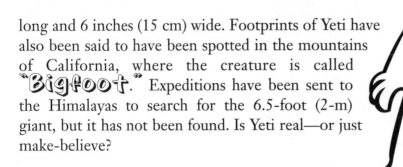

long and 6 inches (15 cm) wide. Footprints of Yeti have also been said to have been spotted in the mountains of California, where the creature is called "**Bigfoot**." Expeditions have been sent to the Himalayas to search for the 6.5-foot (2-m) giant, but it has not been found. Is Yeti real—or just make-believe?

Mountains and Weather

Mountain ranges have a strong effect on air movement, rain, and snowfall. When warm air moves up the *windward* (windy) side of a mountain, it cools. The air loses some of its moisture by *condensing* (turning into a liquid) and falling onto the mountain as rain or snow. Once air has moved over the top of a mountain, it has lost most of its moisture. The *leeward*

Mountains affect the weather by forcing air to move over them. The moist air rising up the winward side of a mountain brings rain, while the air moving down the leeward side has lost its moisture and is dry.

(away from the wind) side of the mountain is much drier than the windward side. Tacoma, Washington, which lies on the west (windward) side of the Cascade mountains, gets an average 37 inches (94 cm) of rain every year. On the other side of the mountains (the leeward side), the city of Yakima averages about 7 inches (18 cm) of rain per year.

The dry, leeward region of a mountain range is called a "rain shadow." Deserts are often found in rain shadows. In the United States, the Mojave Desert and Death Valley lie in the rain shadow of California's Sierra Nevada Mountains.

5

Forests

FROM REDWOODS TO RAIN FORESTS

What's the oldest living thing on Earth? One of those giant tortoises at the zoo? No. The teacher you had last year? Not even close. A 2,000-year-old California redwood, so big that a tunnel carved through its trunk allows cars to drive through? Wrong again. The answer lies in a quiet forest high in the White Mountains of eastern California. Bent and twisted with age, the oldest living thing is a bristlecone pine tree named "Methuselah," after a

man in the Bible who is said to have lived to be 969 years old. Scientists have calculated that this tree sprouted from the ground at the time the pyramids of Egypt were being built—4,700 years ago. Standing about 25 feet (7.6 m) tall, with a trunk about 46 inches (117 cm) in diameter, the tree contains a thin vein of living wood within about 90 percent dead wood. Few people know exactly which tree within the ancient forest is Methuselah. Scientists have not marked it because they don't want anyone harming or cutting down the famous pine.

The Forest Ecosystem

From the cool *evergreen* (always green) pine forests of Sweden to the misty rain forests of the Amazon River basin, great varieties of forests are found throughout the world. A **forest** is a large area of land covered with trees. In addition to trees, many other living things make up the community of a forest: plants, mammals, reptiles, amphibians, birds, insects, and millions of tiny organisms that can only be seen through a microscope. Air, soil, and water make up the environment of the forest. Living things, interacting with the environment, make up the **forest ecosystem.** Each member of the forest ecosystem is important for the survival of the other members.

The energy source that drives the forest ecosystem is the sun. The first step occurs within leaves, where *solar* (from the sun) energy is transformed into food for plants. This process is **photosynthesis.** Green plants must have water, minerals from the soil, and a green substance called "chlorophyll" to make food. Sunlight produces a chemical reaction in the leaf that creates chlorophyll and gives the leaf its green color. Together, chlorophyll and sunlight produce sugar and starch from *carbon dioxide* (a gas in Earth's atmosphere) and water. This chemical process creates oxygen as a by-product. Forests are constantly *inhaling* (taking in, as in taking a breath) carbon dioxide and *exhaling* (giving off, as in blowing air out) oxygen.

The ecosystem is also important for every creature's survival. Without the oxygen that plants and trees put into the atmosphere, people and animals would die. Plants are also responsible for removing carbon dioxide from the air. Carbon dioxide is a gas that traps heat in the atmosphere. High levels of carbon dioxide would increase the temperature of the planet and would cause severe climate changes.

In the next step in the forest ecosystem, animals eat the plants. Other animals then eat the plant-eating animals. The remains of all dead animals end up on the **forest floor,** where millions of tiny organisms feed on them. These *microscopic organisms* (too small to see without a microscope) include bacteria and other *protozoans* (organisms consisting of one cell), as well as some *fungi* (plants without leaves or roots, including molds and mushrooms). As they eat, the tiny organisms *decompose* (break down) the dead-animal bodies into various chemicals, such as minerals. These substances then seep into the soil of the forest floor, where they are absorbed by the roots of plants. The plants then use the minerals to create food . . . and the cycle begins again.

Tips for Leafy Greens

Nature's recipe for a forest has two main ingredients: water and a warm growing season. A forest needs at least 15 to 20 inches (38 to 50 cm) of rain per year and at least three months of frost-free weather in the growing season.

EXPERIMENT

PHOTOSYNTHESIS AND STICKIES!

Plants need sunlight to create *chlorophyll,* the green substance that helps them make food through photosynthesis. Chlorophyll appears as tiny green specks along the inside walls of the cell of a leaf. In this experiment, you'll block sunlight from a section of a leaf to see how chlorophyll is *not* made in the shade!

What You Need:
• A potted green houseplant

• A small paper "sticky" (such as Post-it note)

What to Do:
1. Place the sticky on one of the leaves near the top of the plant.
2. Set the plant in a spot where it will get direct sunlight.
3. Keep the plant in the same position for five days.
4. Remove the sticky.

What Happens and Why:
The area covered by the sticky paper faded to a lighter shade of green. Without sunlight, the cells in the leaf were not able to create chlorophyll. Without the green chlorophyll, the color of those leaf cells changed.

When Earth Was Green: The History of Forests

The first forests on Earth appeared about 365 million years ago, at the end of Earth's geological era called the "Devonian period." Giant club mosses (with clublike limbs) and many-leafed ferns arose from the marshy land to a height of 40 feet (12 m). Buzzing through the trees were Earth's early insects.

Five million years later, at the beginning of the Carboniferous period, much of the land was swampy. Tree-sized ferns and club mosses grew even taller, alongside trees with long sweeping leaves called "horsetails." The lush growth provided hiding places for huge prehistoric cockroaches, 𝔰𝔭𝔦𝔡𝔢𝔯𝔰, scorpions, and dragonflies. Dead trees fell to the wet ground, sank, and were buried under many layers of mud. Bacteria or other small organisms could not live in the wet ground, so the trees never decomposed. Their minerals were preserved and, after millions of years, they were squeezed into hard deposits of coal. Today, people burn this ancient black substance, called "fossil fuel," for energy.

About 240 million years ago, in the Mesozoic era, much of the land was drier than in the Carboniferous period, and the swampy forests were gone. *Gymnosperms* (trees that *don't* carry seeds in either a fruit or a seed case) covered Earth in forests of *cycads*, trees with giant palmlike leaves; *ginkos*, with fanlike leaves; and seed ferns.

A new kind of forest began blooming about 138 million years ago during the Cretaceous period. *Angiosperms* (trees that enclose their seeds in fruit or in a seed

Earth's first forests contained giant club mosses; tree-size ferns; and trees with sweeping leaves, called "horsetails."

case) such as magnolias, maples, poplars, and willows appeared. Flowering shrubs filled out the lower levels of the forests. The Cenozoic era, beginning about 63 million years ago, brought a cooler climate and vast flowering and *conifer* (cone-producing) forests across Europe, Asia, and North America. For more than 60 million years, these lush forests covered much of Earth and were home to many types of **birds** and other animals.

Colder temperatures spread *glaciers* (giant sheets of ice) over these forests during the great Ice Age, which began about 2.4 million years ago. (We look closely at glaciers in the next chapter.) Not until the last glaciers retreated, about 10,000 years ago, did forests begin to grow again over North America and northern Europe and Asia. The ancestors of today's forests, these forests grew back to cover about 60 percent of Earth's surface.

After the Ice Age, the next force to take a chunk out of forest land was humankind. People discovered many uses for wood, such as for building homes and towns, and for burning to produce heat. They also cleared forests to make room for fields to grow crops. In addition, during the 1900s, people built factories that put poisonous gases in the air, which killed plants such as trees. This destruction of forests is **deforestation.** Today, only 30 percent of Earth's surface is covered with forests.

City of Trees: The Layers of the Forest

Although there are different types of forests, all forests have the same basic structure. Each forest consists of five major layers, from high to low: canopy, understory, shrub layer, herb layer, and forest floor.

The branches and leaves of the tallest trees make up the forest **canopy.** The type of tree that makes up the majority of the forest is the **dominant tree.** The dominant trees, which receive most of the sunlight, produce the most food in the forest and can form a roof over the rest of the forest. Birds, **insects**, and climbing animals eat the fruit and leaves of the canopy.

Shorter trees that can grow and survive without much sunlight make up the **understory.** Young dominant trees that are on their way to the top also live in the understory. *Shrubs* are

Forest layers.

different than trees because they contain clusters of woody stems, rather than a single trunk. The **shrub layer** of a forest is not very dense because shrubs do not get very much sunlight below the understory, near the forest floor. Birds and insects make their homes in understory trees and forest shrubs.

The **herb layer** contains baby trees called "seedlings," as well as ferns, flowers, and grasses. If the canopy is thick, the herb layer will not get very much sun and will be spare. Walking, sleeping, and slithering on the herb layer are forest animals such as mice, deer, bears, and snakes.

Covered with mats of velvety moss, dead leaves, animal droppings, and the remains of dead trees and animals is the *forest floor.* The forest floor is one of nature's most awesome recycling shops, where nothing is wasted. Earthworms, fungi, insects, spiders, bacteria, amoebas, and other tiny life-forms transform nonliving things into substances that bring new life to the other trees and plants.

Talking Trees: Reading the Rings

Each year, a tree adds a layer of wood to its trunk and branches. In the spring, when water is plentiful, the tree creates new growth cells. These early cells are large, but as the summer moves on and less rain falls, the cells become smaller. In the autumn, *growth* stops. No new cells are produced until the following spring. The contrast between the new and the old cells is sharp enough to create a line when a *cross-section* (a slice) of the trunk is viewed. These lines are **tree rings.** They reveal the age of the tree—one ring for every year—and much more.

A tree produces wider rings when there is an abundance of rain. Narrow bands are formed in a drier season. Scientists study tree rings to learn about weather conditions in the past. The study of tree rings to date past events is called "dendrochronology" (from the Greek words *dendron* "tree," *chronos* "time," and *logos* "word"). Tree rings also show the dates of *droughts* (periods with little or no rain), *insect plagues* (massive numbers of bugs that eat practically everything in sight), and even volcanic eruptions. For instance, during large volcanic eruptions, the

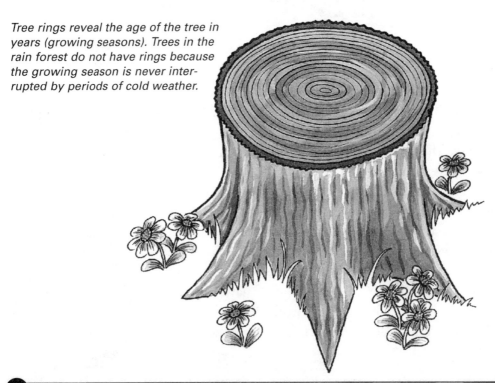

Tree rings reveal the age of the tree in years (growing seasons). Trees in the rain forest do not have rings because the growing season is never interrupted by periods of cold weather.

ash blown into the air can block sunlight and cause Earth's climate to become cooler. Forest growth slows when the temperature drops, and the change in growth can be read in the **tree rings**.

The secret knowledge of tree rings was discovered by Andrew Ellicott Douglass, a professor at the University of Arizona, in the 1920s. By studying the ancient bristlecone pines of the American west, he learned about weather patterns that existed 800 years before Columbus reached the shores of the New World. His student and assistant, Edmund Schulman, studied tree rings of very old trees in Colorado, Nevada, and Utah to learn that a severe drought took place from A.D. 1215 to 1299. The drought may explain why the Anasazi people of the region left their long-established cliff homes. The rings also showed a period of heavy rainfall from 1300 to 1396. Schulman discovered that this pattern of flood and drought repeated itself about every 200 years. This information helps scientists predict long-range weather patterns.

Something for Everyone: Major Types of Forests

Scientists *classify* (group) the world's forests in several ways. Some describe them in terms of the types of trees they contain, such as hardwood and softwood forests.

A *hardwood forest* contains *broadleaf* trees with flat, broad leaves such as oaks, maples, and hickories. These hardwood trees are **deciduous,** which means that they lose their leaves in the autumn and grow new ones in the spring. A *softwood forest* contains *coniferous* (cone-bearing) trees, which contain their seeds inside their cones. Pines, firs, and spruces are coniferous trees with long, narrow, needlelike leaves. The green **needles** are replenished constantly, keeping the tree green all year. For this reason, a needle-bearing tree is called an "evergreen."

Forests can also be classified into six major forest formations that have distinct climate, soil, and moisture qualities. Formations offer detailed descriptions of Earth's widely different types of forests. The six groups are tropical rain forests, tropical seasonal rain forests, temperate deciduous forests, temperate evergreen forests, boreal ("northern") forests, and savannas.

The Rainiest Place on Earth

One of my favorite weather reports for *Good Morning America* was given from the world's wettest spot. On Hawaii's Kauai Island, Mount Waialeale is covered with a rain forest that never stops dripping. The average rainfall on Waialeale is about 585 inches (1,486 cm) per year. I arrived there by helicopter with my camera team and found a clear spot outside the forest to make my weather report. Today's forecast? "Rain," I said. Just then, a few seconds after the camera started rolling, a small cloud just above us opened up and drenched me from head to foot! When I'm right, I'm really right!

Tropical Rain Forests

Wet, misty, and warm 365 days a year, tropical rain forests are located near the *equator* (the imaginary line that separates the top and bottom halves of Earth). This band of Earth is warm all year because it receives the most intense rays of Earth's Sun. In a tropical rain forest, the average yearly rainfall is about 92 inches (234 cm). The annual rainfall is never less than 80 inches (203 cm), and very wet years have received more than 300 inches (762 cm). The broadleaf evergreen trees of a tropical rain forest are at least 98 feet (30 m) high.

Why does it rain so much near the equator? The heat of the sun causes ocean water to *evaporate* (change from liquid water to water vapor). As the warm, moist air rises, it cools. Cooler air cannot hold as much water vapor as warm air, so

Going Buggy

An area of rain forest the size of two football fields may contain 42,000 different kinds of insects.

some of the water vapor condenses into water droplets and forms clouds. Water droplets fall from clouds as rain. (A close look at clouds and rain appears in my book *Can It Really Rain Frogs?*) The constant heat near the equator keeps the process of evaporation, cloud formation, and rainfall going continuously.

The largest tropical rain forests in the world are along the Amazon River basin in South America, the Congo River basin in Africa, and various rivers in Southeast Asia. Tropical rain forests contain the greatest variety of trees of any forest. More than 100 different types of trees can be found in 1 square mile (2.6 square km) of land. Most tropical rain forests have three canopies, with the top one reaching 150 feet (46 m) into the sky. Another feature of a tropical rain forest is its rich growth of vines and *epiphytes*, plants that live on other plants. The woody vines protect the tall trees from blowing over when high winds blow through the tropical rain forest. The epiphytes live directly on the trees and don't have roots going down to the ground. Epiphytes get all their food and water directly from the moist air.

The tropical rain forest looks very thick when viewed from the outside, such as from a river. Plants take advantage of the sunlight that falls on the sides of the forest and fill up all the spaces around the sides. Inside the rain forest, however, there is enough open space to walk comfortably, or even to ride a bicycle! Forest explorers use a *machete* (a large knife) to mark their trail, but they do not need to cut a passage to move through the rain forest.

Tropical Seasonal Forests

Unlike a tropical rain forest, which receives rain throughout the year, the tropical seasonal forest has a definite rainy season and a dry season, as well as a cooler climate in general. This type of forest is found in Central America, central South America, southern Africa, India, eastern China, northern Australia, and the Pacific islands. Somewhat shorter than a tropical rain forest, the canopy of a tropical seasonal forest reaches to about 100 feet (30 m)

Land of the Giants

Tropical rain forests are home to many giant-size life-forms. Even the grass is outrageously tall! Here are a few of the thousands of amazing life-forms that live in the tropical rain forests' warm, moist, and green world.

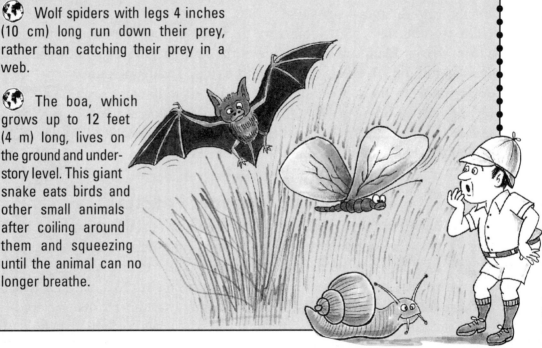 *Bamboo,* a type of grass, grows up to 100 feet (30 m) high. Even more spectacular is the speed at which it grows: up to 36 inches (91 cm) in 24 hours!

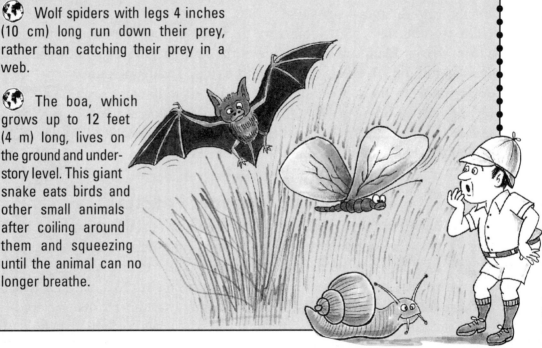 The world's largest flower, the *Rafflesia,* spans 38 inches (97 cm) across and can weigh up to 38 pounds (17.2 kg).

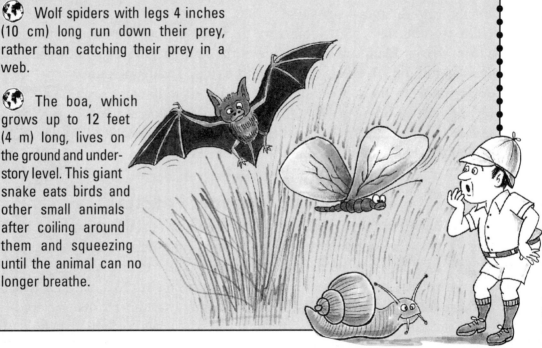 Water lilies as large as tractor tires are strong enough to support a child on the surface of the water.

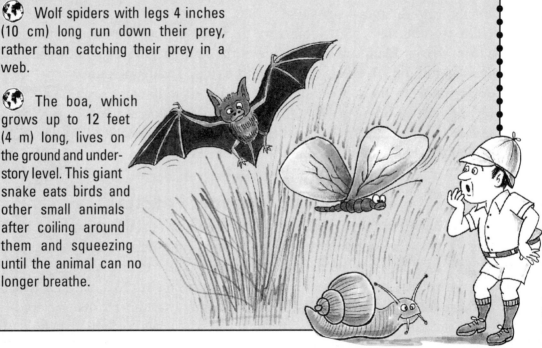 Wolf spiders with legs 4 inches (10 cm) long run down their prey, rather than catching their prey in a web.

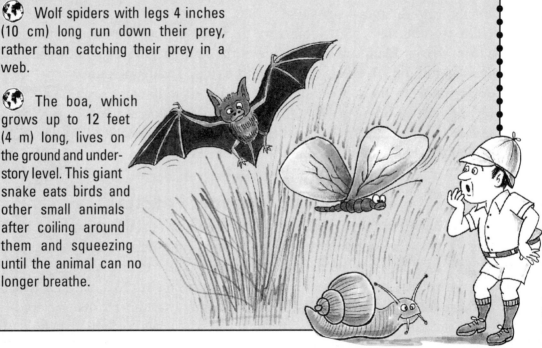 The boa, which grows up to 12 feet (4 m) long, lives on the ground and under-story level. This giant snake eats birds and other small animals after coiling around them and squeezing until the animal can no longer breathe.

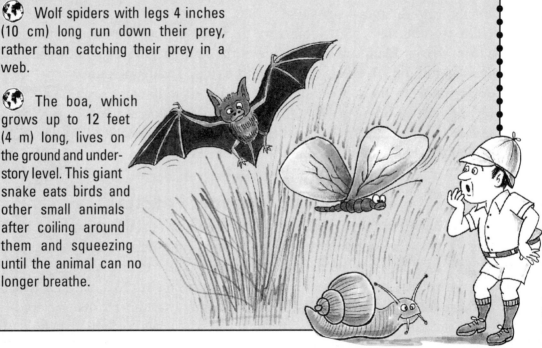 Monster-size moths fly through the forest with 12-inch (30-cm) wingspans. Next time you look at your ruler, imagine a moth that size!

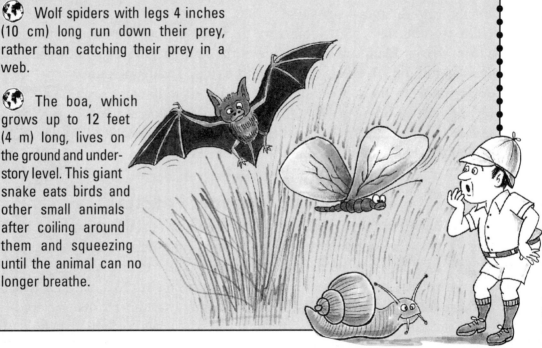 Bats sweeping through the forest canopy for insects can have a wingspan of up to $5\frac{1}{2}$ feet (71.7 m).

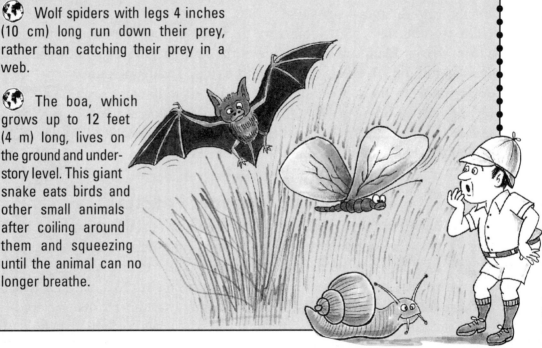 From the tip of its head to the tip of its tail, an *iguana* (a large lizard) can measure $6\frac{1}{2}$ feet (2 m) in length. These green vegetarians are good climbers and spend most of the time about 100 feet (30 m) above the forest floor.

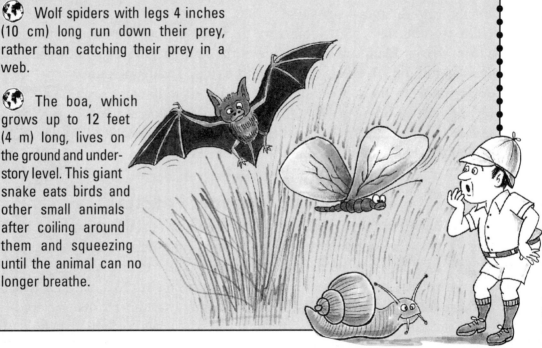 Watch your feet! Forest snails can grow to be about 15 inches (38 cm) long!

above ground. This forest also contains many deciduous trees, which lose their leaves during the dry season.

Temperate Deciduous Forests

Forests filled with broadleaf deciduous trees are found in regions where there are *temperate climates* (warm summers and cold winters). As the temperature begins to drop in the autumn, the forests blaze with orange, red, and yellow leaves that will later fall, leaving the deciduous trees bare in winter. In the Great Lakes region of the United States, these forests are actually a mix of deciduous and evergreen trees. With canopies that reach about 100 feet (30 m), temperate deciduous forests are found in eastern North America, western Europe, and eastern Asia. Wildlife that lives in these forests includes deer, bears, and wolves, as well as birds that fly south to warmer weather in the winter months.

Temperate Evergreen Forests

Along coastlines that get plenty of rain and mild winters, forests grow with a wide variety of trees. The temperate evergreen forests along the coasts of Oregon and northern and central California are home to the giant **redwoods,** also known as *sequoia.* These evergreen, coniferous trees have been growing for more than 3,000 years and rise to heights of 350 feet (107 m). Redwoods contain soft, reddish wood, which was used to build California's earliest towns and cities and to provide railroad ties for the railways in the American west. Temperate evergreen forests are also found on the southern coast of Chile, the western coast of New Zealand, and the southeastern coast of Australia. In addition to coastal areas, this type of forest grows in the cool climate of the lower mountain slopes of Europe, Asia, and western North America.

Boreal Forests

The dominant trees of *boreal* (northern) forests are evergreens with needle leaves, such as pine, fir, and spruce. Boreal forests grow in climates with cold winters and a short growing season. The structure of a boreal forest is the most simple of any forest, containing one uneven layer of evergreens. Moose, bears, foxes, owls, beavers, and many other animals live in the boreal forests of northern Europe, Asia, and North America, as well as the high mountain slopes of those continents.

Savannas

An area of widely spaced trees over a region that has dry soil and low annual rainfall is a *savanna*. On savannas, trees grow in clumps or are spread out from one another, and shrubs and grass grow in patches on the ground. The largest savannas in the world are found in Africa and Australia. The African savanna is home to large animals such as giraffes, zebras, lions, and tigers.

Tree Tribute:
The Importance of Forests

Forests play an important part in the environment and provide many things that make our lives better. When it rains over a forest, the soil soaks up the water like a **sponge**. This sponge effect prevents water from running over the land and *eroding* (wearing down) Earth's surface. Forest soil filters the rainwater and provides fresh stores of *groundwater* beneath Earth's surface. This ground-water feeds streams, lakes, and wells. The water held beneath the forest provides fresh water for people even in dry seasons.

People use wood from forest trees for lumber to build homes and other buildings, as well as furniture and thousands of other products. Even the paper of this book was made from trees. In many countries, people also burn wood to provide heat for comfort and for cooking.

Tropical forests are also a source of many types of food, such as bananas, pineapples, cocoa, coffee, and other fruits and spices. Cinnamon, for example, is made from tree bark.

Half of the medicines we use are made from plants, many of which are found in the rain forests. Aspirin, a drug used to relieve pain such as a headache, is made from a substance found in the bark, leaves, and roots of a variety of plants. The U.S. National Cancer Institute has listed more than 1,400 tropical forest plants that have cancer-fighting qualities. Rosy periwinkle, a plant from the forests of Madagascar, is used to create a drug that fights cancer and is very effective against some types of children's leukemia. Trees also offer many other kinds of medicine.

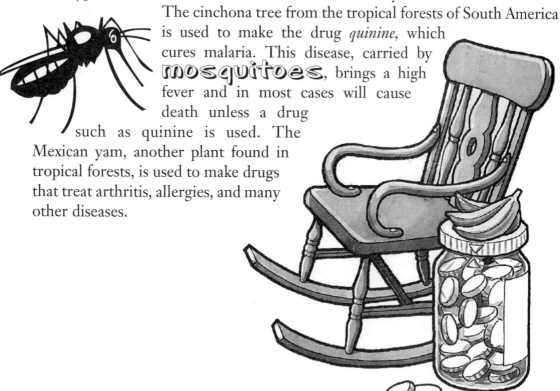

The cinchona tree from the tropical forests of South America is used to make the drug *quinine*, which cures malaria. This disease, carried by mosquitoes, brings a high fever and in most cases will cause death unless a drug such as quinine is used. The Mexican yam, another plant found in tropical forests, is used to make drugs that treat arthritis, allergies, and many other diseases.

6

World of Wonders

Glaciers and Icebergs
FROZEN MAJESTIES

When things get hot and sticky in the summer in New York City, many people travel out to the beaches of Long Island to swim. This long, narrow island stretches 118 miles (190 km) into the Atlantic Ocean and is twice as big as Japan's Okinawa island or Hawaii's Oahu and three times bigger than Tahiti. What many of those happy bathers may not know is that the land they're lying on was pushed into place by a glacier about 15,000 years ago.

Long Island is a collection of soil and rock scraped off the northern ridge of the Appalachian Mountains hundreds of miles away. It was nudged southward by a **glacier**; a large body of moving ice formed on land. When the glacier melted and shrank, the huge mound of earth it had shoved toward the Atlantic Ocean stayed behind as Long Island. The deposit of soil and rock left behind when a glacier retreats is a **moraine.**

Glaciers Get Around

Glaciers have left their mark in a big way all over the world. The Matterhorn, the Swiss Alps' most famous sharp peak, was carved by glaciers. Norway's amazing **fjords,** deep inlets leading out from the mountains to the sea, were formed by glaciers. The truck-size boulders I walk past in Central Park were carried hundreds of miles by a massive sheet of ice.

Glaciers covered 30 percent of Earth's surface at the height of the great Ice Age, which spanned from 2 million to 10,000 years ago. During the Ice Age, giant ice sheets advanced and retreated about 20 times, putting the big freeze on most of North America, Europe, and Asia. An ice age consists of long periods of very cold weather, set apart by a few thousand years of warmer weather. Changes in Earth's *orbit* (path around the sun) were probably responsible for the cold periods of the Ice Age. During the colder eras, Earth was farther from and tilted away from the sun. This position brought less warmth to the planet, so Earth's temperature decreased. When Earth moved closer to the sun, temperatures warmed up, and glaciers melted.

f all of this happened thousands and millions of years ago, how did scientists figure it out? The record of Earth's climate is kept in layers of Earth's crust. Scientists date the rock through *fossils*, imprints and other remnants of plants and other organisms. Rock that does not contain many fossils reveals an ice age, when few living things could survive the freezing weather. Scientists can also calculate what Earth's orbit was like at any time in the past. They have found that the cold and warm periods of the Ice Age match up with the changes in Earth's orbit during those times.

Glaciers no longer rule the northern continents. Unlike the **dinosaurs**, however, they haven't been wiped off the face of the earth. About one-tenth of Earth's surface is currently covered by glaciers. They can be found on mountains all over the world, from Alaska to Africa. The biggest glaciers—95 percent of all glaciers—are found on two land masses: Greenland and Antarctica. The two massive glaciers that cover Antarctica are bigger than the United States, Mexico, and Central America combined. Built up over millions of years, these glaciers are amazingly deep. Imagine ten Empire State Buildings stacked on top of one another: That's the depth of Antarctica's ice in some places, forming a sheet more than 15,000 feet (4,572 m) deep.

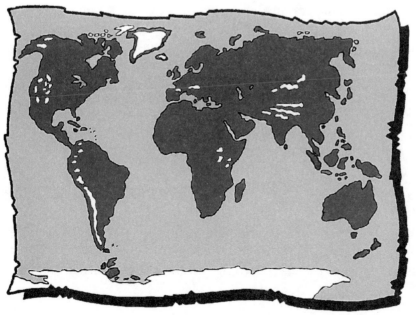

Today, the largest glaciers are found on Greenland and Antarctica, and small ones lie on high mountains throughout the world.

When Is Water Not Watery? When It's a Rock!

The life cycle of a glacier begins with snow crystals. A *crystal* is a solid object with a naturally repeating pattern and a regular shape. A *mineral* is a natural solid object with a definite chemical makeup and structure. Because ice is a crystal, it is also a mineral. A *rock* is a solid natural object made up of one or more minerals. Ice can therefore be called "rock." Because ice consists of a single mineral, it is a *monomineralic rock* (the Latin word *mono* means "one").

Let It Snow, Let It Snow, Let It Snow: How to Make a Glacier

For a glacier to become as thick as a stack of skyscrapers, a lot of snow must fall. A glacier can only develop in a place where the temperature remains at or very near the freezing point (32° Fahrenheit; 0° Celsius) year-round. When snow falls in this type of climate, most of it remains frozen. With each new snowfall, a new layer of snow covers the ground. Years go by, and the layers pile up. The weight of the upper layers on the deeper snow creates a change in the lower layers.

Like a piece of delicate lace, a snow crystal contains tiny points and spaces filled with air. In fact, 80 percent of a snow crystal is air. In a glacier, the pressure from upper layers squeezes together the airy crystals in lower layers. In these lower layers, the points of the snow crystals break as they are crushed by the layers above. When the temperature of the glacier rises above freezing, parts of the snow crystal melt and dribble down toward the center of the crystal. When the temperature of the glacier drops again, the crystal freezes once again—in a different shape. The crystal loses some of its air when the water moves into those spaces and freezes.

The same thing happens when you grab some snow and pack it into a snowball. The heat from your hands melts some of the ice, and the pressure of squeezing the ball breaks and crushes the crystals. The snow becomes more icy and hard as you squeeze it.

When an ice crystal survives at least one summer without melting completely, and loses about 50 percent of its air, it is given a new name. This type of ice is **firn,** the German word for "last year's snow." The creation of firn is the second step (after snowfall) in creating a glacier.

The third step occurs when firn loses even more air. New snowfall puts more weight on the lower layers, squeezes the firn together even more, and pushes more air out of the crystals. When an ice crystal contains only 20 percent air, it is considered an **icy grain.** Finally, when the crystal contains less than 20 percent air, the icy grain becomes **glacial ice.**

Glacier growth depends on the climate. Firn transforms into glacial ice in Alaska, for example, much more quickly than it does in the Antarctic. Alaska's climate creates many snowfalls during the winter and an increase in temperature during the summer, which allows some of the snow to melt. This temperature change *compacts* (squeezes together) the crystals more and more with each snowfall and turns the firn into glacial ice in about 30 to 50 years. In the Antarctic, very little snow falls because the air does not contain enough moisture to create clouds and ice crystals. The bottom of the world may not get a lot of snow, but when it snows down there, it really sticks! Antarctic snow that gradually turns into firn can take as long as 3,500 years to turn into glacial ice.

The development of snow into glacial ice goes through four stages: snowflake, firn, icy grain, and glacial ice.

Ice on the Move

A glacier is defined not only by the type of ice it contains, but also by what it does. For ice to be a glacier, it's got to move! A glacier moves in two ways: through basal sliding and through plastic flow.

Basal sliding is caused by a paper-thin layer of water or water-soaked *sediment* (tiny pieces of rock) beneath the glacier. The bottom of the glacier melts from the underlying heat of Earth, and from the heat given off by friction as the glacier scrapes against the ground. (*Friction* is the energy released when two objects rub against each other.) The enormous weight of the glacier also adds to the melting. Pressure from the heavy weight creates friction in the ice and makes it melt. The glacier slips across the ground along the watery layer.

The second process that can make a glacier move is **plastic flow,** or **creep.** The structure of the ice crystals, which form into flat, thin sheets in the thickest part of the glacier, create plastic flow. The weight of ice

Ice crystals slide against one another to cause the plastic flow of a glacier.

EXPERIMENT: ICE GETS THE SLIP!

Basal slipping is one of two ways that glaciers move. In this experiment, you will put some weight on a piece of ice, to create friction within the ice. In this way, you can observe how friction melts ice under pressure more quickly than ice that is not under pressure.

What You Need:
- Two plastic or glass saucers

- Two ice cubes

- A 5-pound (2.3 kg) weight from the school science lab, a heavy brass doorstop, or a heavy rock with a flat surface.

What to Do:
1. Place the saucers next to each other and upside down.
2. Place an ice cube on each saucer.
3. Place the weight on top of one of the ice cubes.
4. Check the experiment every 10 minutes for 40 minutes.

What Happens and Why:
The ice cube beneath the weight melted more quickly than the other ice cube, due to the friction created in the ice cube and between the ice cube and the plate. This process is what causes glaciers to move along melted water through basal slipping.

from above puts pressure on the inside layers, and they slide against each other. Imagine a fresh, new **deck of cards** sitting on your palm. As you press down on the top of the deck with your other hand, the slippery cards move around. This is how the heaviness of glacial ice makes the ice slip over itself. The movement is not very fast—glaciers move about 1 to 2 inches (2.5 to 5 cm) a day. The world's largest glaciers move more by plastic flow than by basal sliding. The force of plastic flow is so powerful that very thick ice can even move uphill!

In the early 1900s, Swiss and Italian scientists conducted an important glacier experiment in the Alps. They drilled holes through the ice and placed iron rods into the holes. When they checked on the rods over a period of years, they discovered that the rods bent at the top. This proved that the ice at the top of a glacier moves more quickly than the ice near the bottom, which is slowed down by friction as it drags along the ground.

Runaway Glaciers

Most glaciers crawl along at the rate of a few feet per year. Sometimes, however, a glacier will **surge** (speed up) at speeds of 100 feet (30 m) per day! **Glaciologists** (scientists who study glaciers) do not fully understand why glaciers surge. The drainage system of a glacier may be responsible for some of the movement. Usually, meltwater below the glacier drains away through cracks and tunnels in the ice. If the cracks and tunnels become clogged with mud, rocks, or sediment, water builds up beneath the glacier. This provides a slippery surface on which the glacier can slide more quickly.

The center part of a glacier moves more quickly than the ice at the glacier's edges and bottom. The sides and bottom of the glacier are slowed down by friction as they rub against the ground and the walls of neighboring glaciers. An experiment by nineteenth-century Swiss scientist Louis Agassiz (1807–1873) proved that ice in the middle of the glacier moves faster than the ice at the sides. Louis planted a row of wooden stakes across the entire width of a glacier in the Swiss Alps. One year later, he returned and found that all the stakes had moved down the valley, but the stakes in the middle of the glacier had moved the farthest.

Other factors also influence glacial movement. Thicker glaciers move more quickly than thinner glaciers. A glacier flowing down a steep mountain will move more quickly than a glacier spreading out on even land. Temperature also controls the speed of a glacier. Glacial ice moves faster in a warmer climate because it produces more meltwater beneath the glacier.

The Structure of a Glacier

As a glacier flows over uneven land, the ice near the top of the glacier can break into a **crevasse** (a deep crack). The ice deep inside the glacier is more compact than the surface ice, so it bends rather than cracks. Crevasses are a hidden danger to people and animals walking on the surface of a glacier. A thin layer of icy snow on the top of a glacier can hide a crevasse. Some crevasses have been measured to be 150 to 200 feet (46 to 61 m) deep. When I visited Portage Glacier near Juneau, Alaska, in May, 1994, with my *Good Morning America*

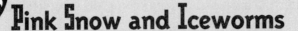

Pink Snow and Iceworms

At first glance, a glacier looks icy and lifeless. If you move your face down close to the surface, however, you'll be surprised to discover tiny organisms that make their home in the deep freeze. Some of the snow and ice takes on a pinkish color from billions of tiny, one-celled, pink plants called "algae," which live in the air pockets. Their neighbors include miniature, black snow fleas, insects about the size of a pinhead. Another chilly creature found on glaciers is the iceworm, a dark worm about 0.4 to 1 inch (1 to 3 cm) long.

team, the expert guides kept us a safe distance from the crevasses they had discovered.

A glacier is always gaining and losing ice. Snowfall brings new snow to the glacier's **zone of accumulation.** In this area, the buildup of snow in the winter is greater than the amount melted during the summer. A glacier *advances* (grows larger by expanding outward), when new snow is added more quickly than it is lost through melting.

A glacier loses snow and ice in the **zone of ablation,** often by melting. The melted snow runs off the top or the bottom in streams. Snow and ice are also lost through evaporation. If snow and ice are lost more quickly than they accumulate, the glacier *retreats* (gets smaller).

When the amount of new snow is equal to the amount of snow that is melting, a glacier stays the same size. Glaciologists refer to a glacier's loss and gain of snow as the **glacial budget.** A glacier that is neither advancing nor retreating has a balanced budget and is in a state of equilibrium.

Glacier Types: Two Frozen Flavors

From the broad flat plains of Greenland to the highest mountain peaks, glaciers come in **two** main types: valley glaciers and ice sheets. The life of a valley glacier begins on the upper part of a mountain when snow collects in a **cirque,** a bowl-shaped dent in the mountain. Some of the snow slips into cracks in the bottom and along the sides of the cirque. The snow melts as it touches the inside of the cracks, and then it freezes

200 miles long!!!

again. When water freezes, it expands. The force of expanding ice breaks the rock of the surrounding mountain. For hundreds and thousands of years, the cracks are broken apart many times, increasing the size of the cirque.

The glacier eventually outgrows the cirque and flows over the edge and down the mountain. The jagged *horns* (sharp towers) of many peaks in the Alps and the Himalayas have been cut away by a series of cirques around the peak. Most valley glaciers are less than 2 miles (3.2 km) long. The Hubbard Glacier in Alaska, however, stands out from the crowd at a whopping 200 miles (322 km) long!

Some valley glaciers reach a flat level of low ground after their long, slow journey down the mountain. The glacier then **spreads out** into a **piedmont glacier,** a thin fan-shaped glacier. Valley glaciers can be

The Hidden City of Ice

Somewhere below the frozen crust of Greenland's glacier, a jumble of rooms and corridors is collapsing and crushing beneath the weight of the ice. Back in 1959, a group of United States Army engineers began building a city beneath the ice, called "Camp Century." The purpose of the project was twofold: (1) to build a safe hiding place for missiles, and (2) to study glaciers and the effects of living in a very cold environment. The engineers bored through the ice with huge plows and dug out rooms and tunnels. The ceilings and walls were supported with steel frames and supports. The soldiers who worked in the deep-freeze colony called themselves "ice worms."

The glacier turned out to be too much for the army. Even though the supports were strong enough to keep the rooms safe, the heavy snowfall pressed Camp Century 1.5 feet (0.46 m) deeper into the ice every year! Digging through the hard, icy surface month after month was a major mess. The city beneath the ice was closed down in 1965.

Camp Century 1/2 MILE ↓

MORAINE MAKER

To demonstrate how a glacier forms a moraine, you can substitute a water-filled bag for a river of ice!

What You Need:
- A sandwich-size plastic bag

- A tray with sides at least 2 inches (5.1 cm) high

- Sand

- Water

- A fork

What to Do:
1. Pour a smooth, level layer of sand into the tray, without filling it to the top.
2. Fill the bag with water, leaving just enough room to tie it tight.
3. Place the bag on the sand at one end of the tray and push the bag along the length of the tray to the other side.
4. Lift the bag, and notice the structure made in the sand. Just as a glacier does, the front and sides of the bag created a curved ridge of sand.
5. Set the bag in the center of the tray and poke holes in the bag by prodding it sharply with the fork. Pull the leaking bag back toward the opposite end of your homemade "moraine."

What Happens and Why:
The bag pushed the sand into a curved mound as it passed back through the tray. As the water flowed out, it pooled into a channel behind the moraine. This is exactly what happens when a glacier retreats and melts.

found in the mountain peaks of New Zealand and Iceland, the Himalayas in China and Tibet, the Andes in South America, Mount Kilimanjaro in Kenya, the Rocky Mountains in the United States, the Yukon in Canada, and the Urals in Russia.

The second main type of glacier is an **ice sheet.** The largest glaciers on the planet are the massive ice sheets of Greenland and Antarctica. Greenland's ice sheet is 1 mile (1.6 km) thick in some places, and it covers almost the entire landmass. The ice sheets that covered the land in North America north of the Great Lakes and most of New England during the most recent ice age were so heavy that they caused Earth's crust to sink beneath them. Ever since those glaciers melted 10,000 years ago, the land has been slowly rising, like a spongy cake. The ground beneath Antarctica and Greenland has also sunk hundreds of feet below sea level under the weight of the massive ice sheets. Ice sheets bury entire mountains. In the Arctic regions of Canada and Greenland, mountaintops peek out of flat plains of solid ice. Such a tip of mountain rock is called a "nunatak," the native Inuit word for "island in a sea of ice."

Glaciers leave behind many forms in the landscape, including holes (kettles) that can fill in with rain to become lakes, as well as huge boulders and long, hill-like moraines.

What Does the Ice Age Have to Do with My Mashed Potatoes?

The sweet corn, potatoes, and other crops from the farms of the midwestern United States wouldn't be on grocery store shelves if there had been no ice age. The rich soil, filled with minerals that make plants grow, was deposited by glaciers.

Crawling, Crushing, and Carving: How Glaciers Leave Their Mark

Inching down the side of a mountain or spreading out over an entire continent, glaciers are awesome natural wonders. The mighty ice rocks of the great Ice Age have left a wide variety of marks on the surface of Earth.

As a glacier scrapes along the surface, it picks up **till,** a mixture of soil and rock. Till builds up in heaps at the front and forward sides of the glacier and is deposited in mounds when a glacier retreats. At the beginning of this chapter, we learned that a deposit of till, such as Long Island, the big deposit off the eastern coast of the United States, is called a "moraine." As a glacier melts and retreats from a moraine, it forms a channel of water that curves along the edges of the moraine. Sediments such as till often contribute variety to a landscape. For instance, till that forms a straight, narrow, and smooth hill is a **drumlin.** An **esker,** a long, snaky ridge of sediment, is a landform left behind when a glacial stream dries up. Meltwater streaming from a glacier contains **outwash,** particles of rock and soil. The smallest and lightest material present in outwash is **rock flour.** When rock flour floats in meltwater, the rock flour gives streams a *milky* color.

EXPERIMENT: SCRAPING BY

Armed with rock of all shapes and sizes, a glacier scrapes the surface of the Earth as it moves. In this experiment, you will use sand and ice to see how the mixture scrapes at a solid surface.

What You Need:
- Wooden cutting board or a scrap of wooden board

- An ice cube

- $\frac{1}{2}$ cup (.12 liter) sand

- A small bowl (for the sand)

What to Do:
1. Remove an ice cube from the freezer, and wait for it to begin to melt.
2. Dip the ice cube in the sand.
3. Rub the sandy side of the ice cube on the wooden board, using a circular motion with your hand.
4. Each time the sand wears away from the bottom of the ice cube, dip the cube into the sand again.
5. Continue dipping and rubbing for about five minutes.

What Happens and Why:
Under pressure from the ice, the sand scraped the wood and left scratch marks in the board. This is what happens to the surface of Earth when a glacier moves over it.

The glaciers that crept down the mountains along the western coast of Norway didn't stop once they hit the icy North Sea. They dug deep valleys into the ocean floor. When the glaciers retreated, sea water flowed in the valleys between the mountains, creating sparkling fjords. These glacial inlets are also found on the coasts of Alaska, Chile, New Zealand, and western Canada.

Known as the "Land of 10,000 Lakes," Minnesota is dotted with water-filled **kettles** formed during the Ice Age. Each lake was created by a block of ice that became buried in outwash sediment beneath the glacier. When the glacier retreated, the exposed ice block melted, leaving behind a hole. Eventually, the hole filled up with rainwater or was fed by an incoming stream, creating a sparkling natural lake.

Glaciers also create another change in the landscape: **erratics,** boulders and other rocks that glaciers move from place to place. These huge rocks are carried and eventually dropped by the ꟽ𝕠𝕧𝕚𝕟𝕘 𝕚𝕔𝕖, often finding new homes in distant places. Giant boulders found along the east coast of Britain, for example, came from an area near Oslo, Norway, about 500 miles (800 km) away.

The wind that whips across Lake Michigan and gives Chicago its nickname, the Windy City, flows over a lake that is also a product of the Ice Age. Each of the Great Lakes was formed by ice sheets that covered a section of North America. These ice sheets advanced and retreated several times, digging out tons of soil and rocks and leaving huge craters in the landscape.

Evidence of glaciers is also found on rocks that crossed the path of the moving ice. On Kelleys Island in Lake Erie, rocks are marked with grooves 1 to 2 feet (0.3 to 0.6 m) deep and 2 to 3.5 feet (0.6 to 1-m) wide. The glacier moved like a conveyor belt through the land, slicing whatever it didn't crush or carry.

Ice alone is not hard enough to carve rock. However, glaciers contain bits of rock in many sizes, from powdery grains to huge boulders. The rock bits within the glacial ice can scrape, scratch, and leave their mark on any rock the glacier passes.

Blue Ice

Glaciers and icebergs sometimes contain blue ice. The color can range from a faint hint of blue to a dazzling, deep shade. Glacial ice that appears blue contains no air bubbles. The structure of the airless glacial ice creates its color. Sunlight is made of a *spectrum,* or layers of different colors. When sunlight passes through airless glacial ice, the shape of the ice causes the blue layer of light to bounce off, and our eyes pick it up. The rest of the colors of the spectrum are scattered and cannot be seen. Glacial ice containing air bubbles appears white because the light that bounces between the air bubbles and the ice contains all the colors in the spectrum—which together look white. (The foam on top of root beer looks white for the same reason.)

Valley glaciers permanently change the structure of a V-shaped mountain valley. By boring through the valley, the glacier smooths and widens the valley into a U-shape. Mountain landscapes that have held glaciers are noted for their cirques and U-shaped valleys.

Ice Afloat: Icebergs

When an ice sheet spreads out beyond the land and enters the water, the floating section is an **ice shelf.** The largest ice shelf in the world is Antarctica's Ross Ice Shelf—a stretch of ice as big as Texas! The front of a valley glacier, called its "snout," can also reach beyond the land. When the snout extends to a body of water, large chunks of the glacier break off, fall into the water, and float away. This process is **calving.**

All glaciers, both ice sheets and valley glaciers, calve when they meet the ocean. The ice that breaks off and floats away is an **iceberg.** Only about one tenth of an iceberg appears above the surface of the water. Hidden below is the rock-hard bulk of the iceberg, strong enough to rip through the thick steel walls of a ship. Icebergs have been measured as high as 400 feet (122 m) above the water surface. That's taller than a 30-story building—and that's just the beginning. An iceberg can extend as far as 2,800 feet (853 m) below the surface, making it nearly twice as high (from its bottom) as the world's tallest building, the twin Petronas Towers in Malaysia.

Iceberg and Glacier Dangers

Each year, hundreds of icebergs calve off the Greenland Ice Sheet. The world learned the awesome power of icebergs in these cold waters after the tragedy of the *Titanic* on the night of April 14, 1912. This ship, which was hailed as "unsinkable," glided past a floating mountain of ice that gouged a hole in the ship's steel side. In less than three hours, the ship sank. More than 1,500 men, women, and children died in the freezing water.

To ensure that a disaster like the sinking of the *Titanic* would not happen again, many nations came together to form the International Ice Patrol.

Ships and airplane pilots keep a close watch on the oceans for icebergs, and they radio in reports of iceberg locations. These warnings have prevented many accidents. In the early 1990s, an enormous iceberg, more than 50 miles (80 km) long and 25 miles (40 km) wide, broke away from the Larsen Ice Shelf in Antarctica. The iceberg is being carefully observed by satellites and airplanes to warn boats of its location.

Most glaciers are in remote places, such as high mountaintops and barren Arctic or Antarctic spaces. However, some are found near towns and can present danger to people living in the region. During warmer weather, meltwater can form a lake on the top of a glacier. If the lake gets too big, it can pour over the glacier into nearby areas and flood the land. In Peru in 1941, a glacial lake suddenly overflowed and flooded the town of Huaraz below it, killing 6,000 people.

Another danger posed by glaciers is the ice **avalanche.** An avalanche of falling ice occurs when a chunk of ice from the snout of a valley glacier breaks off and crashes down the mountainside. Such disasters have been witnessed and recorded in the Swiss Alps for hundreds of years. In 1965, a construction crew was building a dam above the town of Mattmark. Without warning, a huge piece of ice from the snout of the nearby Allalingletscher glacier broke loose. In just seconds, the construction camp was buried under the fallen ice, and 88 workers were killed.

Glaciers and People

The frozen majesties of Greenland, Alaska, Switzerland, and other areas of the world are popular tourist attractions. They're also important natural resources for drinking water, for irrigation of crops, and for generation of electricity.

Drinking Water

Glaciers contain 75 percent of the world's fresh water supply. Arapaho Glacier in the Rocky Mountains, a small glacier with a length and width of about 3/4 mile (1.2 km), supplies water for more than 75,000 people who live in the town of Boulder, Colorado. To survive during the dry spells that hit the region of La Paz, Bolivia, the people rely on fresh streams from a nearby mountain glacier.

Scientists are studying ways to move icebergs from the cold northern Atlantic Ocean to coastal cities where the icebergs could be used for drinking water. Tugged by boats and helicopters, a berg could be wrapped in plastic to insulate it and prevent it from melting too quickly. Pipes connecting the iceberg to nearby land would allow the fresh water to get to people and crops.

Crops Irrigation

For hundreds of years, farmers in Switzerland's Rhône Valley have watered their crops with meltwater from glaciers.

Electricity Generation

In Norway, Canada, New Zealand, and the Alps, glaciologists and engineers have produced electrical power from melting glacial ice. By building a dam to control the meltwater, they **harness** the energy of the water as it moves over the dam and through it turbines, to turn that energy into electricity. As mentioned in Chapter 2, this type of power is hydroelectric power (*hydro* is the Latin word for "water").

Glaciers and the Future

When glaciers melt, the level of the seas increases. If all the glaciers in the world melted, world sea levels would rise more than 180 feet (55 m). This rise would put cities that lie near coastal areas—such as New York, Los Angeles, London, Paris, and Bombay—under water. Glaciers will only melt if temperatures in Earth's atmosphere increase, however.

Some scientists predict that **temperatures** may rise in the future because of the *greenhouse effect*. This process traps heat inside the atmosphere. The sun's energy warms Earth, and some of the energy bounces off Earth and shoots back into space. Gases in the air—including those that come from burning oil, gas, and coal—block some of the sun's rays and trap the gases in the atmosphere. These trapped gases cause the air temperature to rise. The U.S. National Academy of Science predicts that over the next 50 to 100 years, temperatures could rise from 2.7° to 8.1° Fahrenheit (1.5° to 5° Celsius). It would only take about a 2° Fahrenheit (1° C) increase in temperature to increase the melting of the world's glaciers. Scientists, political leaders, and others are working together to study the greenhouse effect and to solve the potential problem of global (worldwide) warming.

Glossary

avalanche: a large amount of ice, snow, or soil that suddenly falls from a mountain.

basal sliding: the movement of a glacier as it flows over a thin layer of water.

blowhole: a crack in the rocky surface of a cliff, leading from a cave, through which air and water blow.

calcite: the mineral contained in limestone rock that makes the rock dissolve when exposed to underground water.

calving: the process in which a chunk of ice from the snout of a glacier breaks off and falls into a body of water.

canopy: the top level of a forest.

canyon: a steep, narrow river valley.

cascade: a small waterfall, often found in a series falling on top of one another.

cataract: a waterfall that flows with a very large volume of water.

cave: an opening in the earth, such as on the side of a hill or a cliff.

cave passage: a narrow tunnel in a cave, which carries water between chambers.

cave pearl: a round structure formed inside a cave when dripstone surrounds a piece of sand.

cavern: a very large cave.

chamber: a large space within a cave, formed when water dissolves limestone rock.

channel: a valley through which a river flows.

cirque: a scooped-out area of rock on the side of a mountain, carved by a glacier.

column: a structure within a cave, formed when a stalactite meets and joins with a stalagmite.

constant temperature zone: the deepest, pitch-black section of a cave, in which the air and water have a constant temperature of 56° Fahrenheit (13° Celsius).

creep: *see* plastic flow.

crevasse: a deep crack in a glacier, which opens to the surface.

curtain or **drapery:** a structure in the flowing shape of fabric, which is formed inside a cave via the process of limestone dissolving and then returning to a solid form.

deciduous: a type of tree that loses its leaves in the winter and grows new ones in the growing season.

deforestation: the destruction of a forest.

delta: a wide, flat area of land making up the mouth of a river as it empties into a sea.

dome mountain: a section of Earth's crust, which has been pushed up by forces beneath the surface and eroded by wind and rain, to expose rock layers of the crust.

dominant tree: the type of tree that is most common in a forest.

drainage divide: an imaginary line along the top of a mountain range, dividing it into two regions of rainwater drainage.

drapery: *see* curtain.

dripstone: the mineral calcite after it has emerged from a drop of water; the substance that creates all the formations inside a cave.

drumlin: a straight, narrow, smooth hill created by material left behind by a glacier.

erosion: the process by which water or wind wears down a substance.

erratics: rocks carried by a glacier and left behind when the glacier retreats.

esker: a landform created by a glacier, in the shape of a snaky ridge.

estuary: the wide, deep mouth of a river.

fault-block mountain: a structure formed when huge blocks of Earth are pushed up along a *fault*, a crack in Earth's crust.

firn: ice in a glacier, which has been squeezed together and has lost about 50 percent of its air.

fjord: a deep valley inlet filled with seawater, formed by a glacier.

floodplain: the flat, level ground of a river system.

fold mountain: a structure formed when two plates of Earth's crust collide, pushing and folding the rock up above Earth's surface.

forest: a large area of land covered with trees.

forest ecosystem: the community of living things in a forest, interacting with the environment.

forest floor: the layer of ground in a forest.

glacial budget: the snow that is lost and gained in a glacier.

glacial ice: ice in a glacier, which has been squeezed together to contain less than 20 percent air.

glacier: a large body of moving ice, formed on land.

glaciologist: a scientist who studies glaciers.

hanging valley: a river or stream channel that flows into a deeper river valley, creating a waterfall.

headwaters: the streams and other water channels that form the source of a river.

helictite: a thin, twisting structure sprouting from a wall or ceiling of a cave, formed by dripstone.

herb layer: the forest layer that contains baby trees, ferns, flowers, and grasses.

iceberg: a large floating block of ice, broken off a glacier.

ice sheet: a massive glacier that spreads out over a continent.

ice shelf: the section of a glacier that extends beyond the land out to sea.

icy grain: ice in a glacier, which has been squeezed so that it contains only 20 percent air.

intermittent river: a river that sometimes dries up completely.

kettle: a scooped-out piece of land, formed by a glacier, which fills with water to form a lake.

lava cave: a hollow space created when lava cools into a tube shape.

limestone cave: *see* solution cave.

moraine: a landform containing soil and rock, formed by the front sections of a glacier.

natural levee: a landform created by flooding along the sides of a river.

outwash: particles of rock and soil carried in the meltwater of a glacier.

oxbow lake: a crescent-shaped body of water formed by a meandering river.

photosynthesis: the process through which solar (sun) energy is transformed into food in the leaves of plants.

piedmont glacier: a valley glacier that fans out onto a flat area of low ground, after flowing down a mountain.

plastic flow or **creep:** the movement of a glacier caused by ice crystals slipping against each other.

rapids: fast-moving water that crashes over rocks in a river.

redwood: a very large evergreen, coniferous tree found along the coasts of Oregon and northern and central California; also called "sequoia."

rill: a tiny, narrow channel of rainwater flowing down a hill or a mountain.

rimstone: a structure jutting up from the floor of a cave, surrounding a pool as a fence would, and formed by dripstone.

river bank: the side of a river.

river basin: the region of Earth drained by a river system.

riverbed: the bottom of a river channel.

river load: the sediment, rock, and other material deposited in a river delta.

river mouth: the area of a river that empties into an ocean.

river source: the place where a river begins, found on the highest land through which a river runs.

rock flour: the smallest and lightest material present in a glacier's meltwater.

sea cave: an opening in a cliff along a seashore.

showerhead: a rare, fanned-out dripstone structure, formed on the ceiling of a cave.

shrub layer: the section of a forest containing *shrubs*, plants with clusters of woody stems.

silt: tiny particles of soil picked up by a fast-flowing stream.

soda straw stalactite: a thin, delicate tube structure, formed by dripstone on the ceiling of a cave.

solution cave or **limestone cave:** an opening beneath Earth's surface, caused by the action of water seeping through rock over millions of years.

speleologist: a scientist who studies caves.

speleothem: any type of structure formed by dripstone inside a solution cave.

spelunker: a person who explores caves.

stalactite: an icicle-shaped structure, formed by dripstone, hanging from the ceiling of a cave.

stalagmite: a narrow, pointed structure, formed by dripstone, rising from the floor of a cave.

surge: rapid movement of a glacier, faster than the glacier's usual speed.

swamp: a wet area of land making up part of some river systems.

till: a mixture of soil and rock picked up by a glacier as it scrapes along Earth's surface.

tree rings: lines visible in the cross-section of a tree trunk, showing each layer of material created during each growing season.

tributary: a river that flows into a larger river.

twilight zone: the section of a cave starting from the mouth of the cave and going as far inside as any daylight can be seen.

unconformity: a missing layer of rock in a canyon, which has been washed away by erosion.

understory: the forest layer containing shorter trees than those found in the canopy.

variable temperature zone: the second inner section of a cave, which does not change as much in temperature as does the twilight zone; *see also* constant temperature zone.

volcanic mountain: structure formed by the action of lava erupting from inside Earth and cooling into heaped-up layers of solid rock.

zone of ablation: the area of a glacier that loses snow and ice.

zone of accumulation: the area of a glacier that gathers additional snow and ice.

World of Wonders

Index

broadleaf tree, 73, 74
brook, 16
butte, 8

C

Cairo (Egypt), 16
calcite, 37, 38
caldera, 12
California, 77
calving, 97
Camp Century, 91
cancer, 79
canopy, 70, 75
canyon, 1–13
    definition of, 2
    making of, 4–5, 8
    See also crater; *specific canyons*
Canyon de Chelly (N.M.), 13
caprock, 8
carbon dioxide, 66
Carboniferous period, 69
Cárdenas, García Lopez de, 3
Carlsbad Caverns (N.M.), viii, 36, 37, 39, 41–42, 44, 45
cascade, 29
Catalina Highway (Ariz.), 7
cataract, 29
cave, 35–47
    color of, 39
    creatures in, 43
    deepest, 44
    glacier, 46
    lava, 46
    paintings in, 47
    sea, 45–46
    sections of, 44–45
    solution, 37–39, 44
    See also specific caves
cave beetle, 43
cave cricket, 43, 44
cave passage, 37

cave pearl, 38
cavern, 36
caviar, 28
Cenozoic era, 70
chamber, 37
Chang Kiang. *See* Yangtze River
channel, 17, 19, 29
Channel Islands, 45
China, 25–26, 46, 61
Chiricahua National Monument (Ariz.), 8
chlorophyll, 66
    experiment, 68
Chyulu Mountains, 46
cinchona tree, 79
cinnamon, 79
cirque, 90–91
civilization, 15
classification, 73
cliff, 45
cliff dwellers, 13, 73
climate, 73, 77, 82–83, 85, 100
Clinton, Hillary Rodham, 52
club moss, 68, 69
coal, 69
Colorado Plateau, 5, 7–8, 9
Colorado River, 4, 5, 8, 10, 12, 20, 21
column, 38
comet, 14
compaction, 85
condensation, 62, 75
Congo River, 75
coniferous trees, 70, 73, 77
constant temperature zone, 45
Continental Divide, 17
Copper Canyon, 2–3
cornice, 52
Coronado, Francisco de, 3
crampon, 51
crater, 12, 14